Inspiring Children to Read and Write for Pleasure

'A marvellous book of great practical value' – James Carter

The lack of int⋯⋯ 372 ⋯ ⋯bers of primary age pupils ⋯qe ⋯ ⋯ches, is a cause for major ⋯ S. ⋯y ⋯ ⋯nts. However, *Inspiring* **Road** ⋯ *Pleasure* fr⋯ ⋯iter, journalist and educ⋯ ⋯red Sedgwick uses the context of literature to illumi⋯ate and inform the teaching of literacy in the primary classroom and inspire children to a love of books.

Aimed at year 4, 5 and 6 primary pupils, but also significant as a transitions text to teaching secondary school pupils, this book shows how children's fluency in language – their thinking, their talking, their reading, their listening and their writing – can be greatly improved and enriched through contact with literature placed in an understandable context. With both focus on prose and poetry, primary pupils will be introduced to using grammar, syntax and sentence construction skills in meaningful contexts. Through the use of inspiring case studies, schedules of work and practical classroom applications as well as literary figures like Dickens, Coleridge, Carroll, Rossetti and Shakespeare, primary school children can enjoy reading and writing again.

With a number of sample passages to use, teaching guidelines and examples of children's work, this book will be of great interest to literacy co-ordinators, practicing Primary PGCE and KS2 teachers and those on BA Primary/BEd courses.

Fred Sedgwick is a writer, journalist and commentator in education. He has written for various national newspapers, education associations and reviews.

Inspiring Children to Read and Write for Pleasure

Using literature to inspire literacy learning for ages 8–12

Fred Sedgwick

Routledge
Taylor & Francis Group

LONDON AND NEW YORK

This first edition published 2011 by Routledge
2 Park Square, Milton Park, Abingdon, Oxon, OX14 4RN

Simultaneously published in the USA and Canada by Routledge
270 Madison Avenue, New York, NY 10016

Routledge is an imprint of the Taylor & Francis Group, an informa business

Typeset in Bembo and Frutiger by
Servis Filmsetting Ltd, Stockport, Cheshire
Printed and bound in Great Britain by
TJ International Ltd, Padstow, Cornwall

British Library Cataloguing in Publication Data
A catalogue record for this book is available from the British Library

Library of Congress Cataloging-in-Publication Data
Sedgwick, Fred.
   Inspiring children to read and write for pleasure : using literature to inspire literacy learning for ages 8-12 / by Fred Sedgwick.
      p. cm.
   Includes bibliographical references.
   1. Literature—Study and teaching (Elementary) 2. Language arts (Elementary) 3. Motivation in education. I. Title.
   LB1575.S43 2011
   372.6—dc22   2010007645

ISBN13: 978-0-415-56505-9 (hbk)
ISBN13: 978-0-415-56507-3 (pbk)
ISBN13: 978-0-203-84532-5 (ebk)

To the memory of John Cotton

1925–2003

Poet   friend   teacher

Contents

Contents

Writing to explore: poems from the written tradition

Acknowledgements

Acknowledgements are due to the following schools:

Aldwickbury Preparatory, Harpenden
Bealings Primary, Suffolk
How Wood Primary, St Albans
Key's Meadow Primary, Enfield
Middleton Primary, Suffolk
Nacton Primary, Suffolk
Peasenhall Primary, Suffolk
Piper's Vale Primary, Ipswich
Riverside Community Primary, Tadcaster
St Michael's Primary, St Albans
Sherburn Village Primary, Durham
Sidegate Primary, Ipswich
Wood End Primary, Harpenden

I am grateful to Peggy Cotton for permission to print John Cotton's riddles on pp.127 and 128.

Thanks to Daniel, especially.

Literature stands related to man as science does to nature

John Henry Newman

Writing is, among things, the place where we can help ourselves cope with the dark parts of our living

John Aubrey

Introduction

But one day I woke up
And the bright light took him away.

(10-year-old writing)

All the colour went out of his eyes and they went grey like pearls . . .

(8-year-old talking)

The local authority built this school in East Anglia – it's not one named in my acknowledgements – in the 1930s. The classroom in which I'm standing, and in which I've been teaching for the past hour has, typically for that decade, glass panels above adult waist level on a wall that runs parallel to a corridor – the kind of corridor you could bowl fast medium pace down, or serve an ace – and the ball would creep the last few feet. A long corridor. A corridor that invites a normal child, who hasn't got, at the moment, a cricket ball or a tennis ball and racket, to run like hell down it, though he (it is probably he) will get into trouble if he does.

Those panels were installed, I'm almost sure, to enable a headmaster (master, of course) or an inspector to watch a teacher's performance. The method for teacher-assessment (though it wouldn't have been called that then) was Keep Your Eye On Them. Spy. The myth was: see how they keep order and then you'll know if they can teach.

But I'm not looking in. I'm looking out from the classroom into the corridor. I'm spying, just as those 1930s headmasters and inspectors were. I'm spying on Jon. He has just been removed from the classroom where I was teaching an Ancient Greek poem, translated into English. All the children were, as far as I could see (and I know I'm biased, but I am also, after all these years, a good judge of an atmosphere) deeply involved. The silence had been broken. The door had opened. 'May I take Jon, Michael, Fatima and Mohammed for their literacy session?' someone had said – parent? LSA (Learning Support Assistant)? governor? – who knows? Nobody had told me to expect anyone. But The Face had peered purposefully, with an air of authority – 'I do this at this time twice a week' – round the door. Not only had a silence been broken, but a spell, too. Jon and the others had put down their pencils and left. The other children had looked up briefly, and then they'd got on with their writing.

That had happened twenty minutes ago, as my lesson was underway. It was clear that neither Jon nor the other four children – nor indeed the teacher – had any choice about where Jon and the others were supposed to be. I'd felt indignant at the time. The children were writing! Writing about a pet that had died! They were studying an Ancient Greek poet! Then four of them had been summoned, and had gone.

Now, from where I'm still standing, I can see them. They are sitting round a hexagonal table with The Face. Each is working through a copy of a little book with no pictures and no conversations, and with no completed sentences: each one ends (I went out to spy for a moment) with underlinings, like this:_____, and the children have to write something on those dashes.

A week later, typing up my notes, I still feel indignant. Jon has a firm grasp on language. He talks and writes fluently and with terrific confidence. His conversation is full of information about his life, and he listens carefully to whatever his classmates and I say. And he thinks, he reflects. Here are some notes I made a while ago following a conversation with him. I'd asked him if he lived near the school:

'Oh, my mum and Dad are divorced, y'know . . . my mum lives over there beside the church . . . My dad lives in _____ [a nearby village].'

There is a sad look up to me. I am much taller than he is, of course, and we are walking around the edge of a playground football match.

Pause.

I say nothing, first because I sense that this is a dangerous area, and second because I want to hear his voice, not mine.

He says nothing. Well, anyway, I reflect, this should be as close as possible to a normal human conversation.

So I say: 'My little boy's mum and dad are divorced too'.

Pause.

He looks up. He nods sympathetically.

'It's very annoying . . . '

There is a long pause here, and then he says:

'Still, I have two houses now, so that isn't so bad . . . and my nanna has a horse at hers, and she lets me ride it when I go there . . .'

This boy needs, almost as much as he needs to breathe, to think about his life and his relationship with everyone and everything in that life: his mum, his dad, his nanna, that horse, his friends, everyone else. And that thinking involves talking about it. And it means writing. All this use of language in its primal use, to speculate, to communicate, is healthy; it will help him to learn about both triumph and disaster, and it will help him to treat those two impostors just the same.

Writing is not a matter of giving children relevant skills, and then, once our records show that they have acquired those skills, letting them write. It is a matter of acquiring those skills through the practice of writing, much as you learn to swim, not through learning swimming skills, but by swimming. No-one would begin to teach a child to swim, or ride a bike, with a theory lesson backed up with a worksheet to ensure that the skills have been remembered. It's down to the local swimming pool, or down to the park with the bike. And writing is a matter of getting pencil, and paper and writing. Under the influence, maybe of an Ancient Greek writer and about a lost pet.

Certainly Jon displays little confidence. It's been squashed flat under a disturbing perfectionism that has damped it down the moment he begins to write. He rubs out letters that don't look perfect. He does this, even, to the capital 'T' of his first 'the', and I can tell that, at some previous school, poor sap, he has been knobbled by a handwriting policy – italic, cursive, whatever – and that he has, thereby, learned something that every handwriting policy (whatever it is intended to teach) teaches: elegance and neatness come before communication. Frequently, before he writes a word, he checks the spelling, sometimes with the teacher, sometimes with me, sometimes with the learning support assistant.

When did Jon lose his confidence? Children like him who stick their hands up, who say 'How do you spell . . .? Or who say 'I'm stuck!' I ask them: 'Do you think a writer puts his hand up when he can't spell a word? Do you think she waits until her friend comes round to get her *un*stuck?', and I suggest that they 'have a go'. But in this school the teacher and the

LSA ask Jon to sound it out: 'Retriever'? 'r', 'e', 't', 'r', 'ee' . . . and so on. And not, especially the last, very helpful, really.

'Disturbing perfectionism' may look like an oxymoron: perfectionism sounds like a 'good thing', and both teachers and parents might well yearn for and then applaud such a trait in a child. But my favourite novels and plays do not seem to me to be perfect. When I listen to a piece of music, I want it to be as technically correct as possible but, more than that, I want to be moved by it: moved to think, moved to laugh, moved to cry, moved, even, to dance.

I wrote earlier 'I'm watching them through this window'. But I didn't, not for more than a minute or two. Here is something more cheerful going on: Ayesha, along with twenty-odd classmates, is inside the room. She is sitting at a desk just behind where I've been spying on Jon. She is not 'doing literacy skills'. (Those inverted commas speak volumes about my misgivings. How do you 'do' a 'skill', let alone a 'literacy' one?) She is writing a poem about an animal. As indeed Jon was, until a few minutes ago, until he was hoicked out of the room. Here is a draft of Ayesha's poem:

> Every day I woke up and I would open his hutch.
> When I picked him up, the way he looked at me.
> When I touched him his silky fur ran through my fingers.
> I loved the way when I held him he tickled me.
> But one day I woke up
> And the bright light took him away.

I loved this poem, but I sensed that there was a problem with the tense in the last line, and talked to Ayesha for some time. This was sensitive matter, but I risked it: 'Did your rabbit die as you touched him for the last time? Or had he died already?' Adults might feel that this was an insensitive question, a kind of inappropriate prying. But Ayesha was not at all troubled by this discussion, and she changed the line to 'And the bright light had taken him away'. I also suggested that she put commas round 'when I held him' in the fourth line.

Literature? Of course. But also literacy. We go back to that word that the stranger had said when she'd come into the classroom where I was teaching this lesson. Ayesha is learning here about the structure of complex sentences, about punctuation, about tenses; though all this is secondary to the substantive learning, which can be loosely called Personal and Moral Education; which is, in fact, learning about life and how to live it and how to express our feelings and thoughts about it.

This is the poem I'd read to Jon and Ayesha and the rest of the class:

A Battersea dog

We got him in Battersea twelve years since.
We loved his bark and the symmetrical prints
   Of his paws
   On shiny floors.
But last week the dark chose him, or he chose the dark.
I listen at night, and I cannot hear him bark.

> (After the Greek of Tymnes (second century BC). Version by Emily Roeves and Henry Burns Elliot, from Sedgwick 2000)

What's going on here in this classroom and in that corridor? To over-simplify for a moment, Jon is studying literacy and Ayesha is studying literature. These are two words with the same Latin root, *littera*, letter. But they have developed variant meanings. The older word, 'literature', is first recorded in the fourteenth century. It has come to mean, among other things, 'the realm of letters . . . the writings of a country or period . . . writings esteemed for beauty of form or emotional effect . . . writing expressing ideas of universal or permanent interest'. Some of these ideas sound overblown now, but there is more than a germ of truth inside them. As John Henry Newman wrote, 'Literature stands related to man as science does to nature'. Literature is the way we understand humankind: ourselves, and our relationship to each other and the world. It is, as Ezra Pound put it in *The ABC of Reading*, 'news that stays news'.

The other word, 'literacy', first recorded in 1883, is a back-formation from 'illiteracy'.[1] It has a far narrower resonance, probably seen best in the context of the Victorian need for low-paid clerks and ladies' maids who could read, write and count: Webster's *New International Dictionary* defines it as 'an ability to read a short simple passage and answer questions about it'. The ubiquity of the word in educational discourse today suggests that our system has moved back towards a view that is reflected in the Victorian experience, the need for clerks, rather than a need for members of our society to understand life in all its complications, in its joys and sadnesses.

So Ayesha, in using her literacy, is exploring her relationship with a rabbit that died and, by extension the relationship of all humankind to kept animals. This exploration involves her intellect and her emotions. So it is, in its small way, in the way of an immature writer (and there will be many immature writers in this book), literature. It is part of a search for a truth. And, crucially, her literacy-learning has a context, one that means a great deal to her.

On the other hand, Jon is 'doing literacy'. The marks he is making on his form bear no relation to his life; have no context. Were he older, this wilfully-imposed tedium might, with some justification, cause him to rebel. But he is only ten, and he is docile as he places his ticks and crosses, his more or less meaningless words, where he thinks they should go. Though he may be using his intellect in a narrow sense, he is emotionally detached from his activity, as anyone would be; much as I was detached last week when filling in my passport renewal form.

It is likely that Jon has made no connection between what he is doing now, and what he does when he writes with me. Years ago I taught in a school which used a Maths scheme written by Harold Fletcher. It was known, therefore, as 'Fletcher' as in 'Get out your Fletcher books'. I was startled when it emerged that the children had not realised that 'Fletcher' was also Maths. I wonder what children think their literacy worksheets are: whether they connect them with the words they think, speak, listen to, read and write every working moment of their lives.

This book is an attempt to re-build a bridge between these two notions, literacy and literature. Its necessary division into two parts (prose and poetry) masks an important truth. All literature, whether written in prose or in verse, or whether responded to in prose and verse, contributes with power to our literacy; to children's literacy, in particular, of course, but also to ours as teachers, learning support assistants (LSAs) and parents. All reading and all writing, in other words, is educational: writing and reading a shopping list may offer low level learning ('We are getting through too much gin', for example; or 'That cat's costing us a lot'); on the other hand, reading and writing in the grip of Charles Dickens, Mary Coleridge or Anon (see below) offers learning at a high level. That all applies whether we are considering prose or poetry.

There is one underlying assumption that has become increasingly impor-tant to me over the years: children's writing is nearly always worth more careful scrutiny than teachers usually give it, so I have tried to honour the children's writing by looking at it with due care.

My central passion in this book (and elsewhere) is children's writing. But a senior adviser made me think hard when she said to me recently that her authority had 'a shortfall in literacy', and that she and her colleagues had identified the problem with oracy. She meant that children were scoring low in the literacy SATs, and that their inadequate speech had been identified as the cause. Her jargon, characteristic of the times we live in, was ugly, but she was, nevertheless, right. It is certain that children in schools everywhere and at every time have had little enough chance to talk. This was obviously true in Victorian schools, where, of course, Silence was Golden. But I know of one primary school today where the headteacher is trying to imposes a silence rule on the children when they walk along the corridors; and even in the best schools, children get too little practice in talking.

I came across 'the rule of two thirds' in a lecture thirty years ago. This rules states that two thirds of the time in the typical classroom, someone is talking; that two thirds of the time, that talk is teacher talk; and that two thirds of that teacher talk should be characterised as administrative or disciplinary, rather than educational. A moment's reflection makes it clear what an absurd state of affairs this is: teachers are (and this is true for LSAs too) almost by definition, as I have said, expert talkers. Their presumed fluency is one reason why they have chosen their profession, or why it has chosen them. Children, on the other hand are, almost by definition, inexpert talkers. They are still learning. They are tyros. But teachers – and LSAs, given the chance – give themselves two thirds of the practice.

In Sedgwick (1997) I give an account of a group of six children left, without an adult present, and with nothing but copies of the song 'Full Fathom Five' from Shakespeare's *The Tempest* and a running tape recorder. I watched them through a window, but couldn't hear what they were saying. Here's that speech:

Full fathom five thy father lies;
Of his bones are coral made:
Those are pearls that were his eyes:
Nothing of him that doth fade,
But doth suffer a sea-change
Into something rich and strange.
Sea-nymphs hourly ring his knell:
Hark! Now I hear them – ding-dong bell.

Later, when I played the tape back, I wrote down some of their comments:

> I thought it was about a statue . . . there's been a shipwreck, you can tell
> because there are fish and there are bones, and there's pearls . . . Pearls come
> in big clams . . . in oysters! . . . yeah, oysters. This is something to do with
> the sea . . . could be a river . . . I doubt it, look at the seaweed . . . could be
> riverweed? . . . what is this sea-change? That's the tides, or it could be some-
> thing has happened to the boat. . . Or it could be he has died, and turned
> into a swarm of fish . . . I think somebody's father was a sailor in a shipwreck,
> and the sea-change is, the weather changed and he got shipwrecked . . .
> Rich and strange, that's the pearls that were his eyes . . . fathom means she
> has found out where her father lies . . .

Note the way the children explore the expression 'sea-change' (usage,
by the way, invented by Shakespeare): how they move rapidly from one
hypothesis to another: 'sea-change', someone suggests, denotes the tides;
then a different voice expresses the thought that it's 'something happening to the boat'; then it's someone 'dying and being changed into a swarm
of fish'. And finally it refers to the change in the weather that caused the
wreck.

But it was a member of a second group of children, all eight years old,
who jolted me when she said, 'All the colour went out of his eyes and they
went grey like pearls . . .' In hundreds of readings of this passage, not to
mention times I've heard it performed on stage and on DVD, this idea had
never occurred to me. And now I feel certain that this child's understanding is close to at least part of Shakespeare's intention. And the question is
raised: how much opportunity would this child have had in the classroom
with all the other children, and, more to the point, the teacher present to
step in whenever she hesitated or stumbled in her speech; thus foreclosing
on the child's learning.

'Oracy' is what my adviser friend would call this. Even though I might
prefer to call it 'talk', we are both concerned about the same issue; and we
would both assume that a teacher is indispensable in any setting where the
aim is for children to learn. It seems obvious to all of us most of the time.
That adviser and I have been trained as teachers, have practised as teachers, are defined by society as teachers. Teaching is what we do. It requires
some leap, and, quite possibly some considerable act of humility, to admit

that children can learn without teachers' presence. Something is going on, something invisible, inaudible, unrecordable, and therefore something of no interest to inspectors and politicians: read the children's words again, and speculate on the thinking going on here.

Thought. As I write, and as my readers read, we should be reflecting on that literally hidden element in literature, in literacy. And that is why, although nearly all of the literature that I have included here leads to children's writing, it can lead to thought and speech, if we give the children time in the lessons (it seems so obvious! But it rarely happens) to think and talk.

As I have been writing this book, I have found that my material divides into three kinds: prose, verse from the folk tradition, and verse from the written tradition. Much of the material was not made specifically for children, and it is important to me that each of 'I remember' by Thomas Hood, 'To the Moon' and 'Waiting Both' by Thomas Hardy speaks to the young even though neither Hood nor Hardy had them in mind as he wrote. The same goes for some of the fictional passages – Charles Dickens, Anthony Trollope and others. And although some of the traditional material was made for children, other parts of it were made for (or even invented during) the pub sing-song.

Part I

Prose

Introduction

I think . . . indeed, I am almost sure . . . but memory is a notoriously deceitful witness . . . that I could read by the time I started infant school. Most teachers would probably say the same. Indeed, one problem that besets the teaching of reading, especially to reluctant readers, is that hardly any teacher has ever been in that poor, word-frightened child's predicament when he or she is ordered to stare at small black shapes on white paper and to try to decode them.

Those of us who became literate early must try to imagine it. You are 7 years old, and you are ordered to convert these meaningless shapes to common sense in an atmosphere that suggests that doing this is the most important thing in the world. It is, in a sense, you are led to believe, a life and death matter, because you'll get nowhere in life if you can't read. But these shapes mean nothing to you, especially when compared with that football that you were belting around that playground ten minutes ago; they mean nothing to you compared to those maggots in the tin when you go with your big brothers to fish in the reservoir at the weekend; they mean nothing to you compared with your ballet lesson, or your birthday party tonight. And yet this big person, sitting beside you in a corridor, is insisting that you have a go. What will happen if I can't do it? you wonder.

We understand this child no more than the nurse at my doctors' practice who has just weaned me off smoking understands the attraction of smoking. She has never sucked on the weed, never gone to bed and been unable to sleep because there was no small cigar in the flat to accompany the morning cup of tea. She has never faced the predicament of the addict with his ludicrous, killing habit. You could say, perhaps, that we need to recruit anti-smoking nurses who have puffed their sixty-a-day and packed it in; and, by the same token, we need to recruit teachers who struggled with print when they were little, and who learnt to love print later. Both tall orders, of course.

Even though I was, at 5 years old, a tyro reader, I was 'put on' (what an odd metaphor is embedded in that phrase! – I must follow it up some time) a reading scheme (Blue Book, Red Book, Green Book, Yellow Book – you know, or can imagine, the kind of thing) and many of the stories that the writers of that scheme published have stayed with me my whole life through. There was the Dutch boy who saved his village from flooding by putting his finger in the dyke; there was Helen Keller and her heroic conquering of her blindness and deafness; and there was Offero who unknowingly carried the Christ child across a stormy river, and who became, as a result, Christoffero and, subsequently, Christopher. That scheme was published in hardback, and that fact, for me, already an infant bibliophile, was part of their charm. Real Books! And I have remembered each of these stories, and I use them with children. Boys called Christopher are thrilled by the last one.

My discovery of the power of the story, like many people's, had had a more intimate beginning: bedtime. 'Talking in Bed' is an emblem, of course, of 'two people being honest', as Larkin put it in his poem with that title (Larkin 1988). Well, that is true in the way Larkin meant: lovers are naked with each other in bed more ways than one, or they should be; but it is also true of parent and child. Most parents instinctively understand the multi-faceted value of conversation at this time: it's calming, as I have said; it is a bond between parent and child; it is a chance to give and receive pleasure; it is (if any parents want to see the matter in such a cold light) a cornerstone for the child's learning of language; and it is a chance for any bad times during the day to be absolved. It has a sacramental quality. It is a chance to be honest.

That was where it all started. But I suppose now that those *Wide Range Readers* (that's what that reading scheme was called! I suddenly remember) made it clear to me that those stories were public; were, potentially at least, in everyone's possession. They were public possessions that we, as members of the human race, shared; stories that were evidence, in fact, of our common humanity.

And later at Sunday School there were Bible stories. I want to stress here the word 'story' rather than the word 'Bible'. Adam and Eve, Cain and Abel, David and Jonathan and the rest were all part of a store of myths that educated people from a Judaeo-Christian background would have known, as much as a previous generation, at least the parts of it educated in public schools, would have known the classical myths – and even my generation, or some of it, and not in public schools, heard about Odysseus and Polyphemus on the classroom radio. It is a truism to say that these stories are no longer significant to children's lives, and the only two Bible stories that nearly everybody knows something about are Noah's Ark and the narrative of the birth of Christ in St Luke's Gospel – and the second is always tinselled up out of all recognition.

They have their own stories now, of course, many generated by media that is largely closed to some of us. But tell them one of the stories listed above with expertise and enthusiasm, and you will give the lie to any notion that children no longer respond to the old media: the human voice accompanied by nothing except, possibly, the illustrations in a book. Or read – or better still tell from memory – the stories in Oscar Wilde's book *The Happy Prince and Other Stories*. The ending of one of them will leave almost any child open-eyed, slack-jawed and, more to the point, *thinking*: 'And they found the giant lying dead under the tree all covered with white blossom'.

Members of the human race have told, and have listened to (and then, at a late stage, written down and read) stories since who knows when. These stories may have had many purposes: to lull a baby gently into sleep; to entertain relatives; to cause laughter and tears; to exhort to a greater effort in battle; but, more importantly, while they were functioning in all these ways, they often helped (whether this was intended or not) both the teller and the listener to understand, and therefore to deal with, some predicament: love, impending but uncertain; love departing; or a battle lost, or a battle to come. Or death.

To call the stories told in the early chapters of Genesis 'myths' is not to call them falsehoods, and therefore it is not to diminish their status, not to belittle them. And to say that they are 'unhistorical' or 'unscientific' is beside the point. They are something other than chronological accounts, or scientific treatises. They deal with humankind's relationship with, to begin with, the void that we assume must have been there before human existence, and which is there before we are born and, possibly, after we die; they deal with the natural environment and our relationship with it; they deal with ignorance (and the other side of that coin, innocence); with sexual love; with knowledge; guilt; with creativity; with how God walks in the garden in the cool of the day.

To take the point of the environment, it has been noted before, but it is still ignored by fundamentalists, that the order of the creation of the world is quite different in the two accounts. The first (Chapter 2:4a) has something like: light, herbs and grass, fruit, sun, moon, stars, animals, man, woman; and the second (the rest of Chapter 2) has: man, plants, rivers, animals, woman. The two accounts were made for different purposes, but neither is intended as a historical or a scientific account. They are theological documents.

I wrote earlier how stories help us confront realities. 'Red Riding Hood' deals with the danger that potentially surrounds all children, and so does 'Goldilocks'. That wolf stands for all the child-murderers (and child-abusers) throughout time. A modern story like Maurice Sendak's *Where the Wild Things Are* deals with temper tantrums in what still seems to be, after all the years since it was published, an original way. The Oscar Wilde story that I mentioned earlier deals with innocence, selfishness, repentance and death among other things, and yet it is open to 7-year-old children

To tell a story is a uniquely human activity. Dogs do not send their young to sleep with picture books, or gather round in bars to swap jokes, or gossip about neighbours. Neither do they read stories in newspapers, or value novels. Orang-Utans, those more civilised of apes, suffer and rejoice, but they do not write stories or tell them to each other, or sing happy or sad songs.

How to wreck the story-writing impulse

Stories told, listened to, written down and read are vital to human emotional, spiritual and intellectual development. So the thought that a child might be about to write one must be exciting. But much schooling does its utmost to drain the activity of all pleasure. It is easy to do this, and it is a day-to-day activity in many schools. A notice on a hundred primary school classroom walls proclaims (or it did until recently):

Here are some ways of beginning a story

Once upon a time there was

It was a dark and stormy night

In a country long ago and far away

There was once a handsome prince

All of these are clichés, and the cliché is the enemy of all good writing. The novelist Martin Amis made this point with characteristic force when he called his 2001 book of literary criticism *The War Against Cliché*. Few readers will notice every cliché on a page (some will, though), but they have a deadening effect nevertheless. But, even more importantly, a writer only uses a cliché when the brain is not engaged. So as teachers we have to ask what learning is going on when a child writes an opening to the story in any of the ways suggested above, when, of course, they are not only using a cliché but one handed thoughtlessly down to them. One might say that no thought is required: in fact, thought is being actively discouraged.

To make children aware of this problem, I composed the beginning of a story with a class of Year 6 children that was, as far as we could make it, entirely composed of clichés. They had to be, I made it clear, not just phrase-clichés like 'long ago and far away', but also situation-clichés like 'his father was a harsh and cruel man'.

It was a dark and stormy night in a strange country long ago and far away. A handsome prince lived in a fine castle with his father and a hundred servants. His mother had died just after he was born, and his father was a harsh and cruel man who lived only for his own pleasures, which were eating, drinking and hunting.

The young prince wanted to show his courage in battle, but his father had promised his son in marriage to a rich old widow who lived in a haunted castle in that faraway land.

Fortunately, the experiment collapsed when a child suggested 'But the prince had discovered Facebook . . .'

For a way of teaching children how to begin stories with sentences that is the opposite of these sentences, see pp.64–66

Here is another deadener from a hundred classroom walls:

You might try some of these interesting adjectives / adverbs

The adjective issue is a troubling one. Indeed, the best prose, and certainly that kind of prose describing fast-moving events, is often spare in adjectives, and children, when pushed to find 'interesting adjectives' often write lists of adjectives that repeat, or get close to repeating, their meanings, and the story becomes logjammed. The obvious example is in the phrase 'dark and stormy night'. Most nights are dark, and certainly all stormy ones are. Read, for example, the novels of Ernest Hemingway, to see how narrative and character development can move to tears with no adjectives and few or no adverbs.

And another related nonsense is this notice on the wall:

Other ways of saying 'said' are:

Answered
Reckoned
Objected
Murmured
Shouted
Commented

I suspect that this notice is a response to a National Curriculum target about 'interesting' verbs. But the reader's interest in a conversation in a novel is *not* in the verbs substituted for 'said', but in what *is* said. Indeed, when tension is required in dialogue, you don't even need 'said', as countless modern novels show (see especially, again, Hemingway, who takes this principle too far sometimes, and you find yourself counting back to the beginning of dialogue to see who's speaking in the middle or at the end).

This book is about helping children to write, and it is largely concerned with great writers. But there are ways of bringing some freshness to children's writing that don't follow on from Dickens, Trollope and the rest.

The first is the trick of asking them to write stories that have exactly fifty words. When I teach this lesson, I introduce three other rules. First, a good story nearly always leaves something unspoken; second, that every word in a very short story must do its work; that, therefore, adjectives and adverbs, counter to the current orthodoxy in literacy teaching, are fat, while verbs and nouns are muscles and bones: they enable creatures to stand up (nouns, bones) and they enable creatures to move (verbs, muscles). I suggest that the children will probably come up with a first draft of sixty or seventy words. This leads to what is almost always a valuable experience: the consideration of every word to see if it is pulling its weight.

The third rule is to give some thought to the length of sentences. An effective story will probably begin with a short sentence, because almost every reader finds a long, multi-claused sentence off-putting at the beginning. Add to this the odd fact that if you mix long and short sentences, you will get a reputation for a good style.

Two 12-year-olds produced this working together. I like to think of the thinking and talking that went on as they drafted and redrafted, as they considered words and cut some away:

The new pupil

The classroom door opens. All eyes turn. No-one dares to giggle or laugh. The new pupil is introduced to the class and to the teacher by the head-master. Will she cope? Will she get on here?

It will be a test of her maturity. The wheelchair is put in place.

Fifty words there: I've checked. And no room for 'said' or 'opined' or 'remonstrated' or 'argued'; and no room, either, for any adjectives or adverbs, except for 'classroom' and 'new', which the writers could hardly have avoided.

Another way of getting children writing narrative that doesn't depend on literature, other than their everyday reading, is to ask them to begin a novel.

Children are almost always keen to get to the action straightaway. This exercise is about setting a scene, and demonstrates as practically as possible how valuable putting off the action can be. You simply tell the children that they should describe a room where their main character lives or works, and make sure that the room tells us about the character. Here is an example:

There I was. I stood in an old house by the entrance to a room. I thought I could hear the house creak. A heap of dust fell out. I stood back and let the dust pour out. Once I had stopped coughing I went into the room. The room was so old and dusty my thoughts seemed to echo round it.

As I stood there I noticed a distinctive feature in the corner. It appeared to be the only thing in the room not covered with a three centimetre layer of dust. It was very well cared for compared to the rest of the room.

You may think this strange but this was an old oak clock dated 1795. As I moved near to it, more things became visible through the thick clouds of dust. There were carriage clocks, grandfather clocks, fob-watches and all sorts.

I swept all the dust away from the corner of a huge mahogany table. There was a book. I opened it, and in the middle of the first page in big old-fashioned writing it said 'Repair Record 1783'.

The book was old and fragile, so delicately I turned a page. And there was a person with the same name as me.

(Sarah 10)

This writer is telling us something with that casual-seeming, unemphasised repetition of 'dust'; and her ending is a terrific coup.

Note

Perhaps I am making this book for writers as well as teachers. I don't mean professional writers, though some might well be professional. I mean those who have understood that the act of making an object with words – a poem, a piece of prose, a page of notes out of an event, a distressing one, perhaps – makes the thing more comprehensible than the event it describes. You can bear – just about – looking at these words on the page, but you can't bear . . . what you can't bear, the raw memory of the event.

There are people, and I am one of them, who react to the joys and horrors of life – the birth of a child, the death of a parent, the end of a marriage – by scribbling words on paper, or by tapping away on a computer screen. When things are bad, I have found that writing is a large cog in the machine that helps me to survive. It is often too painful to think about the loss itself. But thinking about what verbal shapes you have made from that loss, and then changing the shape of that material until it seems to say exactly what you wanted it to say, until you know you are telling the truth . . . that is easier, and even comforting.

I'd say to those who never write, think about prayer, think about meditation, think about walking in the park thinking, thinking . . . and writing your prayer or your meditation or your walking-thinking down. That is what I mean about 'writers' at the beginning of this note.

First, though, the nonsense of Samuel Foote.

1

Absolute nonsense!

So he went on a desert island and bought a freckled cow

(10-year-old)

I found the first extract while I was looking for something else in *The Oxford Dictionary of Quotations*. For stage actors (and, of course, all actors were stage actors until the beginning of the twentieth century and the invention of film) memory is a vital matter. When the eighteenth-century actor Charles Macklin bragged that he could memorise anything, the play-wright Samuel Foote made up the following nonsense passage and, in order to test his claim, challenged Macklin to get it by heart:

So she went into the garden to cut a cabbage-leaf, to make an apple-pie; and at the time a great she-bear, coming up the street, pops its head into the shop. 'What! No soap?' So he died, and she very imprudently married the barber; and there were present the Picninnies, and the Joblillies, and the Garyalies, and the grand Panjandrum himself, with the little round button at top, and they all fell to playing the game of catch as catch can, till the gunpowder ran out at the heels of their boots.

(Samuel Foote)

Whether Macklin succeeded (I bet he did) is not recorded. I read this passage to children, and ask them to write something equally daft or, even better, something dafter. I ask the children to do this task in pairs: I am mindful, first, of the value of the learning that goes on in conversation (much neglected in these days when measurement of individuals is deemed all-important). And, second, I am mindful of the fact that two children might dodge the common sense policeman – more of him in a moment – more adroitly than one.

There were two tiny goats and a thousand angels loved them. But the bus was late as usual and all the time the clouds sang their slow tunes like elephants snoring, and while they did only the peace of the fishes comforted them, and they sat playing Monopoly badly. Though the rosemary in the front garden grew and grew and the grass went red and all the calendar dogs pleaded for forgiveness. 'Oh sweet heaven!ly Oh sweet beach! Give me another chance!'

And the bus came.

(Two anonymous boys aged 11)

She went into Antarctica to go and see her best friend. A big dinosaur comes up and kills her. Next, she finds herself on top of the cloakroom with a pencil in her ear. A tiny rabbit comes along and throws a black carrot in her eyes. She walked into Pluto with puffed up cheeks that the turkey drug did. She pops her cheeks and blows lots of people out of her mouth.

(William and Chloe 10)

She surfed down the bogy river on a nose hair. He fell into Asda in a kangaroo's pouch (alive!). After that she had a baby dragon on the motorway which got each by a torch, and then got run over by a chocolate horse which was crossing the railway track. Suddenly there was a bang and he found himself and Reception Desk 2 eating a dictionary sandwich, and a tomato fell from a wind chime.

(Lucy 8 and Felicity 10)

I so wish bogies wouldn't turn up, but they do.

So he went on a desert island and bought a freckled cow. Out of the tree came an Australian flying on a shoe, and he married the great coconut dwarf! A lonely cook grated some cheddar cheese. 'Come back fair pen!' he cried, for the tortoise grew whiskers and the puddle played his kazoo! And snitch himself came hovering down on the carrot board. The remote control flowers grew till the great blue stick dog barked and the monkey was a dog after all! There was a great door which play-do men came out of and started playing the Banjolean Otter. And the cow died. The funeral was held on the moon. The Boss came in and said 'Look at this mess! You're hired!'

(Rory and Gregor 9)

This passage anticipates W.S. Gilbert's 'Nightmare Song' in *Iolanthe*. I looked this up when I got home, and it was a short step then to Alice's dream in the opening pages of *Alice's Adventures in Wonderland*.

I am not setting great store by Foote's passage, or by the children's writing in this section. But writing their nonsense while impersonating him will set them free; and if the sceptic wonders what it has got to do with the search for truth, I will argue that this work enables them to write about parts of their sub-consciousness. It enables them to by-pass that common sense copper who won't let them write anything that isn't obvious.

For further ideas:

• Nonsense in poetry in this book

• 'Nightmare Song' from *Iolanthe*

2

Getting rid of common sense

Perhaps I'm making a couple of over-optimistic assumptions here. The first is that everyone who is interested enough to have got this far reads other books: novels, poetry, drama, history, biography. The second assumption is that many of my readers have written themselves. I certainly have evidence that many adults do write, though not nearly so much that they read: 'How do you get your stories / poems published?' people often ask me after lectures. 'I have written some, and I think they are quite good . . .' Or, by email, 'Please will you tell me how to get these published?' I often ask, 'Which poets / novelists do you read?' and, especially in the case of poets, the answer is often 'I don't read poetry, I write it' or some variant of that. But aching to be published is a different thing from writing. It is a form of vanity.

I believe, as I said at the end of my last section, that writing itself is *healthy*. It helps the writer, temporarily, to impose a kind of order on the confusion that the world seems to present. However, that order will be worse than useless unless the writer searches for the truth as he or she writes. Writing is nothing less, and nothing more, than part of a search for truth. Or truths. It is not for decoration and, much as we admire them for their style, Dickens' passages quoted at length later in this part of my book are part of Dickens' search for (and presentation of) the truth; the truth about the vile schools that existed, for example, where boys were dumped like rubbish for 365 days a year and for however many years were left until manhood loomed; or about the realities of genteel lower class life in the London slums: that goose 'Eked out by apple sauce and mashed potatoes' in *A Christmas Carol*, for example: was the word 'eked' ever so tellingly used?

Most times when the conscientious writer tries to write a poem, a story, or even to record a memory of a lost parent or grandparent, a dead hand slaps flatly down on a shoulder, and simultaneously a voice demands: 'Make sense . . . Write in a way that everyone can understand what you say' it says. 'Be obvious'. The voice is like Thomas Gradgrind's (more of whom later): 'Facts alone are wanted in life'. This voice insists that communication is all that matters in writing, and, even worse, communication that is as immediate as a headline. To tell the truth is to make sense.

Well, to make sense is a reasonable enough aim, of course. As readers we need nothing more for the construction of a set of shelves or a floor lamp, though we could often do with a little more clarity. And we demand sense, or we say we do, as well as clarity and vividness and facts, from every newspaper report we read. I write 'or say we do' there because the newspapers that sell most copies often decorate each story with the tawdriest jewellery, speculation.

Here is some common sense which I will try to evade. This is a memory, from around my sixth or seventh year, of a farmhouse Sunday evening in County Cavan in Ireland, where my mother's family comes from:

A. The room was at the front of my grandfather's Irish farmhouse, and it was small. In one corner stood a piano, which had some magic in it, which I was to discover later. Everything on the walls was dark, and the gloominess of the atmosphere was increased by the fact that this was what I will discover was called 'the parlour', a room nobody entered except on Sunday night.

But on the Sabbath, the family gathered here. There was my grandfather, the eldest of eight brothers and sisters, his wife and my uncle Stanley, the youngest, unmarried. My mother played hymns on the piano, and we sang. I was only six, and I loved these times. My English father was there too, smoking Capstan Full Strength. I think that he was pleased that my Grandfather also smoked, though only Senior Service . . .

And the magic in the piano was a pianola. You stuck a baguette-sized, baguette-shaped object, all studded with bumps, in the back of it and pulled a switch to set it going, and it played music! And you sat at the piano, tonking the keys however you liked, and made out you were playing the music! 'Look Mummy!'

I have told it here like it was. But suppose I tell it like it is in my head, now, as I sit here typing on a machine that would have looked like something from the weirdest science fiction all those years ago, adding things that occur to me as I write. This is not common sense, to write as if this is happening now, when it happened more that fifty years ago. This is what is nowadays called 'counter-intuitive'. I am going to let words invite me down alleys that may or may not turn out to be blind ones. But I will be telling the truth. Take a risk!:

> B. This is about 1950. The room is at the front of my grandfather's Irish farmhouse, and it is small. In one corner stands a piano, which has some magic in it, which I am to discover later. Everything on the walls is dark. This is 'the parlour', a room nobody enters except on Sunday night.
>
> But on the Sabbath – who else uses a word like that? – The family gathers. This is my grandfather, Harry, the eldest of eight brothers and sisters. He smokes Senior Service, white packs with navy stripes, and a bearded sailor who is there to kid us that smoking is for heroes. This is his wife, my grand-mother, who once smacked me for carrying the runt of a litter of pigs into her kitchen. Or so my mother told me once. And this is my uncle Stanley, the youngest, unmarried. He frightened me once when I was a teenager with a leer . . . Can I remember the names of the others? May, Gladys, my mother, Irene, my mother's twin, Sadie and Willie.
>
> My mother plays hymns on the piano, and we sing. I am only about six, and I love these times. My English father is there too, smoking Capstan Full Strength . . . I think that he is pleased that my Grandfather also smokes, though only Senior Service . . .
>
> And the magic in the piano is a pianola. You stick a baguette-sized, baguette-shaped object, all studded with bumps, a bit like a Braille roll, in the back of it and you pull a switch to set it going, and it plays music! (I can't think of a word at the moment that fits less snugly into this Irish Presbyterian room in the fifties than 'baguette', unless it's 'transubstantiation' or 'gay' in the modern sense.) And you sit at the piano, tonking the keys however you like, and you pretend that you are playing the music! 'Look Mummy!'

I ask children to write a passage like A above, and then to re-write it in terms of B (present tense) and then as third person fiction. This will, of course, seem counter-intuitive to them, against the grain. It will seem like a lie. What, they might wonder, is going on here? But this activity demonstrates practically that the truth can emerge even more strongly when we play with language. Art is a lie we tell *in order to tell the truth*.

There may well be something lurking inside us that needs to be said, and our obsession with 'making sense' may hinder our saying it. Writing nonsense is a lively way of helping children to shake that hand off. I will say much later about nonsense poetry. This prose example of nonsense is a delight, and, because they feel that it sets them completely free for the duration of their writing, it gets children writing.

Lies

Or we might go further, and suggest children simply write a passage with a string of lies. Here is one that was written as prose. When I first collected it in a book (Sedgwick 1997), the writer and I had made it into prose, which pleased us both (though how much say in the matter she had I wonder slightly guiltily now). Now I recast it in the form in which it was written:

Ten lies about my eyes

My eye can turn right round and I can see my brain and in my brain there are lots of little people working. But in the night when I turn my eyes around the people are sleeping on bunk beds.

Sometimes, when I have no-one to play with at school, I take my eyes out and bounce them up and down and when girls come passing by they scream and shout 'Miss! She's taken her eyeballs out!' So I quickly stuff them back in.

And when I'm bored at home with watching cartoons I take my eye out and throw it out the window and it goes around the world and I see that in other places of the world it is much more exciting because there are aliens trying to take over the world.

And when I feel it [my eye] it feels like a very flat piece of paper so I just get a pencil and write a poem and I call it Ten Lies About my Eyes.

These tissue of lies contains truth about a life where someone thinks about how her brain works; where that someone sometimes has no-one to play with at school; where that someone is sometimes bored; where children tell tales on each other; and where that someone has crazy fantasies. And these lies tell those truth like to a set of clichés could.

The example of fiction as a lie is one that has been put before us in many ways and by many writers. Mr Sludge the Medium, in Robert Browning's poem, asks the novelist 'How many lies did it require to make / The portly truth you here present us with?' Leonardo tells us somewhere that art is a lie told to tell the truth, and his famous cartoon in the National Gallery in London that shows Mary's mother, St Anne as a truly massive woman – she must have been some seven feet tall, and with more strength than most grandmothers as she supports both her daughter and her grandson on her lap: and the figure of Mary is huge, too. These are certainly untruths: no woman, in all likelihood has ever been as large as Anne must be here. But the picture tells a truth about, among other things, power.

The opening of *Jane Eyre* (1847:1996) is a lie. 'There was no possibility of taking a walk that day'. It is a lie because neither the speaker, whom we are about to get to know very well indeed, nor the family in which she lives, have ever existed. But the sentence is a wonderful truth, because it tells us so much: walks were often taken, but today none was possible. The sentence places us immediately in a day when walking was impossible. It hints at more than the weather. Where the speaker lives is, at for the moment, Lowood.

3

Characters

One from Anthony Trollope

'If he sees happiness half a mile off, he will knot it, screw it in a ball, and throw it as far as he can'.

'You don't scare me for I am the fire and you are the ice'.

(10-year-olds)

Children, I suspect, think about prose books as stories and stories only. Why wouldn't they, when the beautiful picture books that are read and shown to them when babies and toddlers are, on the surface, mostly plot. The fact that the characters in the best of them – Max in *Where the Wild Things Are*, for example, are beings whose nature gives pressure to the story impresses them less than the story itself.

But the two sentences from pieces of children's writing above show that they can, when given the opportunity, write about character too; and that they can understand that character description will help to move a story, to make a plot, and can be entertaining.

This is an extract from *Barchester Towers* by Anthony Trollope, who is introducing a central character. There is no need to tell the children the character of this man. Here is my edited version of the passage where the unctuous, hypocritical clergyman Mr Slope is introduced (chapter 4).

Mr Slope is tall, and not ill made. His feet and hands are large . . . but he has a broad chest and wide shoulders to carry off these, shall we call them, growths, and on the whole his figure is good. His face, however, is not especially handsome. His hair is lank, and of a dull pale reddish hue. It is always formed into three straight lumpy masses, each brushed with great care, and cemented with much grease; two of them adhere closely to the sides of his face, and the other lies at right angles above them. He wears no whiskers, and is always perfectly shaved. His face is nearly of the same colour as his hair, though perhaps a little redder: it is not unlike raw beef; beef, however, one would say, of a bad quality. His forehead is wide and high, but square and heavy, and unpleasantly shining. His mouth is large, though his lips are thin and bloodless; and his big, prominent, pale brown eyes do not inspire much confidence. His nose, however, is his redeeming feature: it is pronounced straight and well-formed; though I myself should have liked it better if it did not possess a somewhat spongy, porous appearance, as though it had been cleverly formed out of a red coloured cork.

I never could endure to shake hands with Mr Slope. A cold, clammy perspiration always exudes from him, the small drops are ever to be seen standing on his brow, and his friendly grasp is unpleasant.

Of course, parts of this need glossing, first because of its Victorian context, and second, like much of the prose and poetry in this book, it wasn't intended for children. Once I have explained, for example, 'lank', and the eyes that 'do not inspire much confidence', I show the children how this paragraph zigzags between the apparently complimentary, the back-handed, the sly, and the downright negative. He's 'tall' and not 'ill-made' (he is not, we note, 'well-made'); but his 'broad chest and wide shoulders' seem to exist only to 'carry off' his huge hands and feet. And so on. Sometimes the paragraph starts complimentary, and then descends . . . and descends. 'His forehead is wide and high, but square and heavy, and unpleasantly shining' is one example. I read the passage a second time, and ask the children to call out when any word suggesting dampness comes up. They offer these: 'lank', 'grease', 'shining', 'spongy', 'clammy', 'perspiration' and 'drops'. I usually take the opportunity to discuss the meaning of 'porous'.

I show children a copy of this passage, and discuss it with them. How we can make compliments about someone . . . and then kill them, or at least kill his or her reputation. I point out that the passage is not just an attack on Mr Slope's physique, but also on his moral character. We sense that its clamminess is not the only reason we would not like to shake his hand.

After they have thought and talked, they write, in the grip of Trollope's prose, an account of a grotesque character. Of course, they don't manage anything of the novelist's subtlety:

She has the appearance of a sloth. She has a smell like Chanel No 5, but five million years past its sell-by date. Her face is like a cement mixer that has dried up and broken. She could win a beauty contest if her opponents were dead. Her mouth is so big, it could kiss a thousand men at once. She says that she has never been in prison. True. She has been arrested twelve times though.

(Steven 11)

In another school the results were different. I had visited it for twelve years for two or three days each time, and the children knew me and my methods. They possessed the most richly-stocked library I have ever seen in a primary school, especially in fiction. Someone had framed signed drawings by artists, and these drawings adorned the walls. Because of all this (and because of many other things, I'm sure, that I don't know about) the children had the habits of reading for pleasure, and writing for pleasure too. There is little subtlety here, either in this first writer's prose; but there is evidence that she has read, or has had read to her, I would suggest, some of the nonsense literature I will quote or cite in the first part of my poetry section: Lewis Carroll, Edward Lear and others.

And humour. Most children who attempt jokes in writing fail, at least as far as adults (teachers especially, perhaps) are concerned. But this writer didn't tell me she had written something funny, as children sometimes do as they bring out a piece of writing with a poo or bogy joke in it. I was travelling the class, working the room when she asked me for comments in the usual way on this:

She is fat. There is no other word for it. Fat. The next striking thing about her is her hair. It's so short! She's almost bald. Her eyes are big and bold and they are always jumping about like mental kangaroos. She's dumb. A Tots tv fan could beat her on pre-University Challenge.

Going down to her nose, it's a nice cherry nose – shame about the greasy boil on the end of it. It's so big that if you took it to the cinema it would want its own seat! Her lips are big and smothered with lipstick. She is constantly getting new boyfriends . . .

Her shoulders are wide. Most people would associate that with being strong and a boy, you're not kidding. She once picked up three desks at a time. Unfortunately poor Tommy was on top. We never saw Tommy again.

> Her legs are made completely of muscle. When she runs, it looks like there are lots of millipedes inside her eggs. 'Keep going ladies!' she booms in PE
>
> . . .

I think there are moments of genuine comic invention here, and much as Trollope is not a broad comic, it is his prose that had led to this girl's inventive writing. One of those moments is the greasy boil that would need its own seat at the cinema, and the other is that strange image of muscular legs with millipedes inside them. Of course, the Tommy gag doesn't work, and neither does that imitation of an old-fashioned stand-up's routine: 'She is fat. There is no other word for it. Fat'.

4

Characters: Charles Dickens

A Christmas Carol

There now begins a sequence of passages from the novels of Charles Dickens. Dickens (1812–1870) is a less sly, a more passionate, and an angrier writer than his near contemporary Anthony Trollope (1815–1882), and, in places, he is accessible to children. The first book I'm going to cite here, *A Christmas Carol*, is especially accessible because many of the children will have seen one or more of the several feature films based on it. Indeed, the Muppets version, with Michael Caine as Scrooge, would be an excellent film to show children in school at Christmas time.

In this book, a passage describing an unpleasant character even nastier than Mr Slope occurs in Stave 1. Children can learn from it, among many things, the power of adjectives: that, for example, if they are to be used at all, they are often used best in excess. This makes this an especially useful passage these days when 'interesting adjectives' are such a big deal. Here's Ebenezer Scrooge:

> Oh! But he was a tight-fisted hand at the grindstone, Scrooge! a squeezing, wrenching, grasping, scraping, clutching, covetous, old sinner! Hard and sharp as flint . . . secret, and self-contained, and solitary as an oyster. The cold within him froze his old features, nipped his pointed nose, shrivelled his cheek, stiffened his gait, made his eyes red, his thin lips blue . . . A frosty rime was on his head, and on his eyebrows, and his wiry chin . . .

I ask the children, in groups, to list all the adjectives: there are, I think, fifteen in this short passage. We count them: I read the passage, and at each one the children cry out a number, or give a cheer:

tight-fisted, squeezing, wrenching, grasping, scraping, clutching, covetous, old, hard, sharp, secret, self-contained, solitary, frosty, wiry . . .

Teaching adjectives by seeing them, or putting them in a context, and by playing games with them is far more effective than defiling classroom walls with lists headed, usually with dubious truthfulness: 'Here are some interesting adjectives you might use'.

The following story runs pleasingly counter to the conventional wisdom that all the culture to which children are exposed at home comes from television, computer games and other elements of modern media. When I mentioned Charles Dickens to one class, a girl, Hirem, lit up. Shot her hand up. Knew about Oliver Twist. She quoted, 'Please can I have some more'. She knew about David Copperfield and Little Dorrit. She told me later, 'My Dad loves Charles Dickens' books . . . He reads them to me'. She wrote at great speed, having listened to the description of Scrooge above:

> He was as red as hot lava coming up to your neck. His teeth were as sharp as a knife stabbing you. He was as determined as Osama Bin Laden. His hair was as long as sugar cane. The blood of him was not red but black. You could see blood trickling down his wrinkly chin. If your eyes looked into his eyes your soul would go into his body. His coat looks like you're trapped in a cage and can't come out. The darkness was like crocodiles sniping you. He could be as flexible as spider webs. He would hate children being friends.
>
> Jealousy could burn his blood. His brain cracked his guts and he has no brain.
>
> (Hirem 10)

This was originally unpunctuated, and yet this child, as I guessed, and as her teacher confirmed, knew her punctuation. Why didn't she punctuate conventionally, as she usually did? A moment's thought provides an answer. Hirem let the full stops, commas, paragraph breaks and the rest slip because she felt a need to get down on paper what was in her head. This elemental, urgent need to get it down, to tell it like it is, is very strong when the fire is burning, when the muse, or the unconscious, or the imagination is telling you what to do. It is even strong when you go shopping. Do you punctuate a supermarket list? More importantly, do you bother about grammar when you write to a lover?

What response should a teacher make when faced with writing like this? It opens up an abyss between two demands. Conventional educational wisdom, which seems, to politicians and inspectors, so commonsensical, requires, on the one hand: Correct it! Correct it! What were you thinking of, Hirem? The SATs are coming! Oh dear! On the other hand, the teacher might respond with evidence that she is interested in the life of a child's imagination, and she should say something like this:

> Where did you get the ideas about hair as long as sugar cane? And Osama Bin Laden? This is frightening, Hirem, and I quite like being frightened! Tell me about the flexibility of spider webs . . . Can I have a copy of your writing to show to other teachers?

I had asked the children to describe an unpleasant person, but the unpleasantness mustn't, I insisted, be tight-fistedness:

> Mr Dark Fire
> He was an envious man. His eyes were red like fire. He was out of his mind. His name was Mr Dark Fire.
>   He lived alone in an abandoned old wrecked house. He was like a bomb and if anyone made him angry he would count to destruction before he would let it out.
>   He had no wife no kids no one. He was his own person. And if anyone wanted to sell him something like chocolate he would tell them to get off his doorstep and throw the chocolate on the door step and step on it.
>
> (Anon 10)

> She was a backstabber, talked and talked, wouldn't even try to understand emotion. She would wriggle and worm, squiggle and squirm, her way into others, finding the worst in everybody. Hateful, careless, unaware of feeling, ruthless and conniving, she looks blankly towards the moon and says 'You don't scare me for I am the fire and you are the ice'.
>
> (Anya 10)

What a note for a character study this second example is, swerving as it does from everyday language to the poetic and then to the abstract. It goes so far as to cause some concern about what person Anya has met to inspire such writing, but it is, of course, almost certainly, what Keats called 'the truth of the imagination' that has inspired her, as well as her reading. For the latter, it is noticeable, for example, that she has used her experience of picture books: 'She would wriggle and worm, squiggle and squirm'. Her ending is a remarkable, chilling climax. I can't imagine what reading has led to that sentence.

In another school, I taught this passage again. I asked the children to note especially how conversational Dickens' style was here; how he grabs your lapels with that 'Oh!', and how he doesn't let go of them. I also emphasised his similes: 'sharp as flint' and 'solitary as an oyster'. The first writer was used to me teaching poetry, and she began, almost out of habit I suppose, to write in stanza form. Her character is one of those people of whom a friend of mind used to say 'If you've got a black cat, he's got a blacker one':

> Oh how she was vain.
> With a mirror for companionship
> And a comb for family.
> She ignored everyone else
> So we ignored her.

She shoved and she pushed and she scrabbled to be first, in the spotlight. All her life was wasted, wasted in the mirror.

> 'I've got a dog!'
> 'Well I've got a horse!'
> 'I'm going to London!'
> 'Well I'm going to Hollywood!'

She was like that all the time. One step ahead, she needed to be the best all the time.

> Oh how I despise her.
> You're lucky you have not met her.

(Anon 10)

This next one I have included mainly because of its startling climax, though this writer also does conversation well:

Gosh! You should see Mrs Grot. She is mean as can be. She has flaming red hair, you think it's going to reach and strangle anyone. Her thoughts are as loud as a lion's roar. When people say her name in public a cold shiver comes up your spine and freezes at the top of your head, it's like it can't go away. Her eyes were like . . ., um, let's see, oh, I know, a fly flicking one way to another.

Well, Mrs Grot had children of her own but, mind you, she deserted her children. When I went there, they were skinny as dead sticks and so quiet you barely heard them breathing.

Now Mrs Grot had some smashing looks but they had faded away after she had children.

I can't tell you anymore cause she will have a go at me, you may wonder why she might have a go at me, well, you can keep a secret, can you? She's my wife.

(Sophie 10)

One child, Sam, reminded me of H.L. Menken's definition of Puritanism as 'the haunting fear that someone, somewhere, may be happy' (Rodgers 2005). Sam wrote of her character, 'If he sees happiness half a mile off, he will knot it, screw it in a ball, and throw it as far as he can'. This sentence is worth examination. This writer has grasped an idea that most professional writers would at least consider: an old misery would feel that happiness in the distance has to be dealt with. But then it dawns on Sam that, if she lets her imagination work, there is more going on here than she had at first thought. So she squeezes new phrases out of the situation. 'He will knot it', she writes, and 'screw it in a ball, and throw it as far as he can'. Some writers never learn this lesson. There's more to say here than what you've said so far. Think.

This is very like Dickens. See how he takes the cold in the Scrooge passage, and develops it: it 'froze his old features, nipped his pointed nose, shrivelled his cheek, stiffened his gait, made his eyes red, his thin lips blue . . . A frosty rime was on his head, and on his eyebrows, and his wiry chin . . .'

I imagine Dickens giving himself times of silence while he thought, while he allowed his imagination to move in his heart and brain. And I never teach writing without imposing some silent times on the children for thought: 'Please put your hands over your eyes, and think hard: how might your person behave? What might s/he be like? Think . . .' These silences are necessary for the imagination to work freely, and we can see some of its fruits in Sam's sentences, and these following: 'He is so destructive he could cause the apocalypse by himself'; 'He was like a dark night with an axe'; and 'She had a mouth as tight as a cork in a bottle of champagne'.

I want to ask my readers if they could write, in an hour's session, sentences as vivid and as original as these. I couldn't.

For more ideas and examples:

- Ask children to look at the novels of Roald Dahl, and see how he introduces characters like Verucca in *Charlie and the Chocolate Factory* and the Twits in the book of that name. Also, the schoolmaster in *Danny the Champion of the World*, and the farmers in *Fantastic Mr Fox*.

- Ask the children to find a character in a book they have read, and see how the writer introduces a character.

A Christmas Carol

Christmas dinner at the Cratchits'

> Uncle as happy as he could ever be swinging me round and around
>
> (10-year-old)

So far, the characters' studies I have used with children have been of two unpleasant but memorable individuals, both brilliantly named, Ebenezer Scrooge and Obadiah Slope. This next passage is a study of the character, we might say, not of an individual, but of a family. It is a picture painted vividly on Christmas Day; painted, perhaps, by a sentimental Hogarth, if one can imagine such an artist, or a Brueghel warmed by strong Flemish ale on a winter's night. It is important in the context of the whole novel because it provides a dramatic contrast to the picture of Scrooge that I have already quoted, that 'squeezing, wrenching, grasping, scraping, clutching, covetous, old sinner . . . solitary as an oyster'. This is a happy family: even though it is poor, it is a *family*. Everyone shares willingly in the work of producing the meal, except Tiny Tim, who, being a cripple, can't, and his father, who must look after him. It is not a family used to good things, and when good things happen, it is a family that makes the best of them:

Such a bustle ensued . . . Mrs Cratchit made the gravy (ready beforehand in a little saucepan) hissing hot; Master Peter mashed the potatoes with incredible vigour; Miss Belinda sweetened up the apple sauce; Martha dusted the hot plates; Bob took Tiny Tim beside him in a tiny corner at the table; the two young Cratchits set chairs for everybody, not forgetting themselves . . .

There never was such a goose. Bob said he didn't believe there ever was such a goose cooked. Its tenderness and flavour, size and cheapness, were the themes of universal admiration. Eked out by apple-sauce and mashed potatoes, it was a sufficient dinner for the whole family . . . everyone had had enough, and the youngest Cratchits in particular, were steeped in sage and onion to the eyebrows! . . .

Hallo! A great deal of steam! The pudding was out of the copper. A smell like washing day! That was the cloth. A smell like an eating-house and a pastry-cook's next door to each other, with a laundress's next door to that! That was the pudding! . . . like a speckled cannonball, so hard and firm, blazing in . . . ignited brandy, and bedight with Christmas holly stuck into the top.

Oh, a wonderful pudding! Bob Cratchit said . . .

Further accounts of meals can be found in:

* Ask the children to find accounts of other meals in books. Mrs Beaver prepares a memorable one in *The Lion, the Witch and the Wardrobe* by C.S. Lewis.

I haven't taught this passage yet. But when I do I will point out, first, the power of the list in descriptive writing. Indeed, other people's lists, discarded in supermarket trolleys, fascinate me. They give a snapshot of a household's life, like this one, salvaged from a used trolley at my local Sainsbury's:

Berries, Bananas, Ciabatta, Houmos, Steak rump, Chicken breasts, Livers, onions, potatoes (Desirée), Worcester sauce, Large tomato for stuffing, Salad, rice, mince, Ecover, Green sponges, Fresh kipper, Lemon, Halloumi, Potato peeler, whisk, crème fraiche, toilet rolls

It is easy to think of lists as boring documents, but they aren't. There is a story to be told, or at least a word picture to be drawn from that one. And here is one of Dickens' lists. All the family in the first paragraph are named alongside their tasks. This has a cumulative effect, and we see that this is a large family (though it isn't large by Victorian standards) and, as I have said, that every member works hard for each other. There's Mrs Cratchit, Master Peter, Miss Belinda, Martha, Bob and his special charge, Tim himself . . .

More suggestions can be found in:

- Lists in Poetry from the *Written Tradition*, p.00.

There is also the power, as so often in Dickens, of similes. There were two examples in the earlier passage: Scrooge was as 'solitary as an oyster' and as 'hard and sharp as flint'. The first is probably original, the second not, but it is still powerful. I will ask the children to find the similes in the new passage, because they learn about what similes will do far more clearly if they find them for themselves. There are three that have lost none of their force, despite all the changes in London streets since Dickens wrote. The Cratchits' house on Christmas morning smells 'like washing day', and also 'like an eating house and a pastrycook's next door to each other'; and the pudding is like a 'speckled cannon ball'. The last, anyway, presents no problems to modern children.

★★★

I have taught this passage now:

I am in a village school on the outskirts of the county town where I live. I have asked the children to describe Christmas dinner at their house. I've read them the Dickens, and asked them to write as vividly as possible about their memories of Christmas, or about their perfect Christmas, or perhaps a mixture of the two. We've discussed all these similes, and I've asked them to close their eyes and remember or anticipate . . .

As they write in this beautiful silence, I walk around the room, watching their prose passages grow. I am on the alert, as always, for something strange, something original, something daring.

Here are two examples:

The clean cloth was laid out on the table. The smell of bubbling roast turkey was drifting round the room. 'Is it nearly ready yet?' I asked as the sizzling Yorkshire pudding was coming out of the oven. I and my sister Anna laid mats, knives, forks and spoons at everyone's place. Then mummy laid crackers out too. 'Beep beep!' The roast potatoes are ready! . . . Now we could enjoy our Christmas dinner near the Christmas tree once more! After dinner mummy and daddy washed up the Christmas cutlery . . .

It was snowing this Christmas. We put on a hat and some gloves and a big thick coat and went out to build a snowman . . . we made a few snow angels. You lie in the snow and kick your arms and legs sideways . . .

(Erin 10)

For more Christmas poetry:

• Erin's twin sister Anna is represented in Christmas poetry in this book.

This account is unusual. There is a grammatical assurance, unusual in Year 6 children. For example, there's that easy use of the subordinate clause, 'as the sizzling Yorkshire pudding was coming out of the oven' and of the subordinate phrase, 'forks and spoons at everyone's place'. There are no misused present participles (see the next example for plenty of them). I have to make no corrections.

There is also a certain conventionality in 'It was snowing this Christmas': this child is ten. I dug about in my memory – had there been a snowy Christmas Day in my memory, let alone hers, in our part of the country? And that conventionality was also visible in 'mummy and daddy washed up the Christmas cutlery . . .' I was reading a 1950s Ladybird book; though possessing a microwave oven. The only place where this writing takes on life is in the words about snow angels.

By contrast another child writes:

Sprouts bubbling and bouncing in the pan. Children drueling (*sic*) over the desert. Dad sizzling the Yorkshire puddings and cooking the meat. Parents talking loudly while drinking wine. Mum spreading out the cloth on the table. Children opening presents, jumping with joy. Uncle as happy as he could ever be swinging me round and around. Auntie helping mum setting the table.

George and me running around the tree nicking the chocolates then running off.

Smell of warm Christmas pudding melting on the plate.

All out in the snow.

Chickens wondering what snow is. Cats not bothered at all. Dogs rolling in the grass, getting covered in snow.

What more could you have for a perfect Christmas Day.

(Jessica 10)

I was pleased with both of these pieces of writing. Erin's stately prose, with handwriting to match, was a pleasant surprise, but in Jessica's piece I sensed the pleasurable, worrying pandemonium of a family gathering. Though Jessica had left out her main verbs, and though she had invented words ('drueling'), I felt I was there, albeit with that dubious snow again. Erin's writing is impeccably correct; it is neatly dressed in smart casual. Jessica's, though a grammatical mess, is exciting. And it is riddled with misused present participles: bubbling, bouncing, sizzling, talking, drinking, spreading, opening, jumping, swinging, helping . . .

The present participle presents an interesting problem in children's writing. Rather than write 'flames flicker', most children will choose 'flames flickering' when they write, say, about a bonfire. Jessica's penultimate paragraph would read more strongly changed to 'Chickens wonder what snow is. Cats are not bothered at all. Dogs roll in the grass, and get covered in snow'. And her first sentence could be redrafted to read 'Sprouts bubble and bounce in the pan'.

I suspect that the present participle feels safer to most children; the verb in its form 'roll' commits you as a writer: when you use it, you have made something happen.

But even in Jessica's free-flowing work, there are lapses into conventionality. Although that uncle is utterly convincing as he swings Jessica around, as are 'George and me running around the tree nicking the chocolates then running off', the children 'jumping for joy' are not.

A week later, I had thought more about this passage. With a different class, I emphasised similes, and collected ones that the children wrote, all either over the top, or massively conventional. I give the overdone ones first:

Roast spuds like golden rocks of treasure . . . the rustling of presents' rapping paper is like the foxes in the bushes at the end of our garden . . . when we've gone hard core sledging on Dunstable Downs it's like a world unknown to mankind . . .

To over-write is a good stage for a child-writer to pass through, as I will argue shortly.

The clichés included: 'We shoot downstairs like a bullet'. Now this phrase is massively bad; first because, yes, it is a cliché; but what makes it even worse than most clichés, which have become clichés because they are true (news often does travel 'like wildfire', for example) this one is simply not possible to visualise at all.

I had noted a Christmas motif in the Dickens passage. Bob, the father, looks after Tiny Tim. There is someone central to the scene at Christmas. Someone is vulnerable, a baby in the cradle, a cripple, or, as here, a treasured relative:

> At Christmas it's very manic at my house. In the morning I run downstairs and meet my brother in the kitchen, not daring to go into the lounge. Our kitchen is like a chef's house in a little room. My brother and I crack on with breakfast, making scrambled eggs and toast.
>
> Usually my granddad and grandma come round on Christmas Eve and spend the week with us. My grandma is called Joyce and my granddad is called Roderick. We write lists about what we think Santa has brought us for Christmas.
>
> Dinner on the other hand is very different. I set the table while my mum cooks the turkey. Then I rush into the lounge to see if my grandma is OK. My granny is ill you see. Her words get muddled up. She was OK. I took my granny by the hand and led her into the kitchen. Then she said to me 'That was nice very!' I knew what she really meant.
>
> (Amy 10)

For further resources:

• Yet if His Majesty, or sovereign Lord, p.133–34.

Setting a scene: *Nicholas Nickleby*

> Their bodies split with pain, their minds unhinged
>
> (10-year-old)

When modern children 'do' Victorian England, they hear about the sufferings of 6-, 7- and 8-year-olds who struggled in workhouses, schools and factories in the nineteenth century. Teaching this period is especially important in primary schools because it teaches this generation of children that children have always been abused. You can sense the empathy that the children feel with the boys in Dotheboys Hall in *Nicholas Nickleby* when you read to them the passage I have quoted below.

Victorian England and its social history are easy to research. Google, google, google, of course. But sometimes teachers decide that children will take part in re-enactments of Victorian schoolrooms. A 'headmaster' in a black gown shouts at them. He sends one, dunce-headed child, to sit in a corner. It is always a boy, in my experience: a weird sexism rules that suggests that boys are more suited to this kind of pretend cruelty than girls, still, in reactionary minds, 'the weaker sex'. He moves others up and down the class as they answer questions rightly or wrongly. 'Girl no. 27' the gowned headmaster barks: 'Move to 18'. I have seen children genuinely frightened in this situation.

One such occasion especially unnerved me. The master – gown, cane, perpetual scowl and all – was played by a member of a two-man 'theatre group', and a hapless boy, dressed in cut-off trousers and a cloth cap, was played by the other man. The first actor was so convincing in his unpleasantness (though not necessarily in his authenticity) that even this experienced teacher felt nervous about what he would do to the 'boy', his colleague, next. Other children – many from cultures remote enough from modern Britain, let alone the actor's travesty of Victorian England – were noticeably frightened, and many of the children were having some difficulty in retaining a distinction between the actor's depiction of the boy and their own situation.

The following two passages of Dickens will teach much more than such fun and games, which have seemed to me, once or twice, to seem to be wish-fulfilment fantasies by teachers ('Those were the days!' is always said by someone) or the antics of frustrated actors (oh, I'm on the stage now, but no-one will boo or hiss).

The first, is, of course, an extreme case, but Dickens knew such places. It comes at the moment in *Nicholas Nickleby* when the innocent hero first sees the horrors of Wackford Squeers' Yorkshire school:

> But the pupils – the young noblemen! . . . Pale and haggard faces, lank and bony figures, children with the countenances of old men, deformities with irons upon their limbs, boys of stunted growth, and others whose long

meagre legs would hardly bear their stooping bodies, all crowded on the view together; there were the bleared eye, the hare-lip, the crooked foot, and every ugliness or distortion . . . There were little faces which should have been handsome, darkened with the scowl of sullen dogged suffering; there was childhood with the light of its eye quenched, its beauty gone, and its helplessness alone remaining; there were vicious-faced boys brooding, with leaden eyes, like malefactors in a jail . . . [Nicholas] could not but observe how silent and sad the boys all seemed to be. There was none of the noise and clamour of a school-room, none of its boisterous play or hearty mirth.

I explained the irony of 'the young noblemen' and we discussed words like 'countenance' and 'deformity' to make their meanings clear. One child knew about hare lips, and also knew the meaning of the word 'stunted'. The words 'faces that should have been handsome, darkened with the scowl of sullen suffering' made an impression on the children, as will be seen from the writing quoted below.

I asked the children to think about different kinds of classroom: some disfigured by anger, or poverty, or caught in the crossfire of a civil war. I pointed out how Dickens used many adjectives. And I suggested that Dickens was never a restrained writer, but one who gladly went 'over the top'. I also told them that Dickens had been a journalist, and that he had seen schools like the one that he describes here, and that seeing these schools made him angry. This writer uses both his lists and his adjectives in a Dickensian way:

Their faces, scarred and cut.
Where eager children should have stood were enemies, separated by
diabolic war.
Never stopping, hacking, destroying each other, crimson blood staining the
walls.
Children of hell, demonic, chaotic, never to cease.
Pure hate blackened their souls, their demented forms broken to bone.
A veil of darkness destroyed all that was left, separating child, welcoming
demon.

Eternity wars, stripping child.
Blood of the child spilling

Minds forever locked away, only battles, till comes death.

Vortex of evil, gateway to hell had unlocked, possessing all.

Their bodies split with pain, their minds unhinged.

They were welcoming death, begging, all their hopes now gone.

Disease and famine in young children, so easy to penetrate.

Bodies that should be living life healthy lay pale and limp, barely clutching
on.

(Rory 10)

This was written in the week of Remembrance Sunday, and media coverage of the Service of Remembrance has seeped into Rory's mind. And he has certainly taken Dickens' over-writing seriously! This kind of exuberance is part of a necessary phase for a writer. If a child-writer is to learn about the dangers of exaggeration, of linking adjective after adjective in a sequence before almost every noun, s/he has to experience the pleasure of playing with words in this way first. And, as Dickens repeatedly shows, over-writing has its place. Even so, if I had had the chance, I would have suggested that Rory take out some of the adjectives. I did it anyway, later:

Their faces, scarred.

Where children should have stood were enemies, separated by war.

Never stopping, hacking each other, blood staining the walls.

Children of hell.

Hate blackened their souls, their forms broken to bone.

A veil of darkness destroyed all that was left, separating child, welcoming
demon.

Stripping child.

Blood of the child spilling

Minds forever locked away, only battles, till comes death.

Vortex of evil, gateway to hell had unlocked, possessing all.

Their bodies split with pain, their minds unhinged.

They were welcoming death, begging, all their hopes now gone.

Bodies that should be living life healthy lay pale and limp, barely clutching
on.

(Rory adapted by me)

I think that this is a good example of 'less is more'; though probably Rory is too young to be taught restraint. And here is someone else writing with no restraint:

> You could actually see the fleas jumping from boy to boy. Their solemn eyes hold the memories of scars that were engraved into their skin. Their weedy necks held the shape of decay with its extra iron limb or cast, and their heads always whispered, as if they were begging for it, Death Death Death.
>
> (Jasper 10)

I asked this writer if he was going to add more – he usually writes at greater length than this – but he said, with a smile, no, he thought he'd finished. I supposed if you're ten and you've just written 'Death' three times, you want to get on with something else. Another child wrote about a classroom where 'the sunshine was pleading to come in'. It was, she wrote, 'a disaster of a school' but, 'though dark, dull and unfriendly, its spirits are still alive'.

The next passage is a famous description of a certain kind of Victorian schooling, and I haven't thought of a way of using it to help children to writing. But I think it would be a powerful stimulus for talk about schooling, learning and education

> 'Now, what I want is, Facts. Teach these boys and girls nothing but Facts. Facts alone are wanted in life. Plant nothing else, and root out everything else. You can only form the minds of reasoning animals upon Facts: nothing else will ever be of any service to them . . . Stick to Facts, Sir!' . . .
>
> 'Girl number twenty,' said Mr. Gradgrind, squarely pointing with his square forefinger . . . Your father breaks horses, don't he? . . . He doctors sick horses, I dare say? . . . He is a veterinary surgeon, a farrier and a horse-breaker. Give me your definition of a horse.'
>
> (Sissy Jupe thrown into the greatest alarm by this demand.)
>
> 'Girl number twenty unable to define a horse!' said Mr. Gradgrind . . . 'Bitzer', said Thomas Gradgrind 'Your definition of a horse.'
>
> [Bitzer, it has been made beautifully clear, has never been near a horse]
>
> 'Quadruped. Graminivorous. Forty teeth, namely twenty-four grinders, four eye-teeth, and twelve incisive. Sheds coat in the spring; in marshy countries, shed hoofs too. Hoofs hard, but requiring to be shod with iron. Age known by marks in mouth . . .'

Well, *is* there anything else in education but facts?

If so, what else is there?

Going through the five senses, suggest what experiences Sissy Jupe had had of horses.

How do you feel as Sissy did? Write about any animal that you know really well. Use the five senses.

Later on, Sissy and Bitzer will meet on the way out of school. Invent a conversation between them, and turn it into a full-blown row.

Further ideas:

• Ask the children to research the school fiction library, and come up with other schoolteachers. Ask them to put them into two lists: ones they would like to be taught by, and ones they wouldn't. Start them off with the vile Major in *Danny the Champion of the World*.

More from Dickens: setting a scene

'Rain falling, falling, falling, nothing but rain against the dark empty sky'
(10-year-old)

The aim of this chapter is to help children to grab a reader's attention from the very beginning. I read the children an abridged version of the second paragraph of *Bleak House*:

Fog everywhere. Fog up the river, where it flows among green aits and meadows; fog down the river, where it rolls defiled among the tiers of shipping, and the waterside pollutions of a great (and dirty) city. Fog on the Essex marshes, fog on the Kentish heights. Fog creeping in the cabooses of collier-brigs; fog lying out on the yards, and hovering in the rigging of great ships; fog drooping on the gunwales of barges and small boats. Fog in the eyes and throats . . .

I ask the children what they notice about this passage. They always mention the repetition of the word 'fog', but they don't notice, usually, that the passage has no main verbs: it is a list of clauses. So I point this out, and the fact that it contradicts current orthodoxy about what a 'proper' sentence is. Also, the clauses are almost all short.

I ask the children to find out what some of the obscure words mean: 'defiled', 'tiers', 'gunwales'. I tell them that by 'caboose', Dickens means a container, and that a 'collier-brig' is a ship carrying coal.

I ask the children to write a passage about weather, using the same techniques: repetition, listing . . . 'Make your writing feel rainy or sunny or snowy or stormy'. In the town where we were teaching and learning, there had been a severe storm two evenings before. One child's writing begins:

> Rain, rain, rain. Down the back of my neck as I came to school. Rain hammering on my umbrella, rain lying by the roadside, getting into my shoes. Rain on the windows of the classroom, rain all day long, so we stay in at playtimes, at dinner time, and get cross with each other. Rain and wind pull the branches of the tall trees like bullies. Rain, we say to each other, this rain, will it ever stop? . . .

> (Anon 10-year-old)

A 9-year-old wrote:

> Rain. Rain everywhere. Rain beating down on the solid tarmac where I stand. Rain crashing on to the roofs of nearby buildings, dribbling down the wall. Rain falling in thick streaks, making puddles, rippling lakes. Rain everywhere. Rain falling, falling, falling, nothing but rain against the dark empty sky. Rain creeping down my raincoat, splashing on to my shoes. Rain, rain and more rain. Nothing but rain. Rain everywhere.

> (Suzannah)

My computer, of course, holds with the conventional wisdom that every sentence should have a main verb, and has complained with wiggly underlinings about the whole of this. But my computer and conventional wisdom are wrong, as Suzannah shows.

> Wind everywhere. Wind forcing the leaves to block our sight. Wind creeping slowly nearby and suddenly bursting out as a surprise. Wind stealing small things from our hands. Wind trying to confuse us swerving left and right. Wind stopping the sun with deep dark clouds. Wind is a traitor, he thrashes the ice and whips the sun away, as though he was on their side . . .

> (Francesca)

Francesca begins by following my rule: make some sentences without verbs
. . . But look how the breaking of that rule, and the following of the conventional one about the nature of a sentence, shoves her into the making of a metaphor: 'Wind is a traitor . . .'.

The preceding chapter of the same book contains many passages which can be used in the same way to powerful effect. Here Dickens conjures up the filth of a Victorian winter in London in three verbless sentences:

> As much mud in the streets, as if the waters had but newly retired from the face of the earth, and it would not be wonderful to meet a Megalosaurus, forty feet long or so, waddling like an elephantine lizard up Holborn Hill. Smoke lowering down from chimney pots, making a soft black drizzle, with flakes of soot in it as big as full-grown snow-flakes – gone into mourning, one might imagine, for the death of the sun. Dogs, undistinguishable in mire. . .

5

Action: Robert Louis Stevenson *Treasure Island*

Here is a very different writer. Whenever I re-read this novel, this passage always shocks me. I understand the thrill my 8-year-old son felt when I read to him another passage from the same book: 'One step closer, Mr Hands, and I'll blow your brains out'. When I read this passage to children, I let them savour the violence and Stevenson's powerful depiction of it. I enjoy watching their faces as I say the words – it helps that I have it off by heart and use the text only as a prompt. But the passage's emotional power is no reason not to examine it, and how it attains that power. Close examination of texts does not, as the conventional wisdom says it does, destroy them.

> And with that, this brave fellow turned his back directly on the cook, and set off walking for the beach. But he was not destined to go far. With a cry, John seized the branch of a tree, whipped the crutch out of his armpit, and set that uncouth missile hurtling through the air. It struck poor Tom, point foremost, and with stunning violence, right between the shoulders in the middle of his back. His hands flew up, he gave a sort of gasp and fell.
>
> Whether he were injured much or little, none could ever tell. Like enough, to judge from the sound, his back was broken on the spot. But he had no time given him to recover. Silver, agile as a monkey, even without leg or crutch, was on the top of him next moment, and had twice buried his knife up to the hilt in that defenceless body. From my place of ambush, I could hear him pant aloud as he struck the blows.

The children and I discussed this passage. I pointed out the violence and rapidity conveyed in the verbs 'seized', 'whipped', 'hurtling' and 'stunning', and they suggested similar verbs. Someone, on prompting, found the horribly appropriate simile 'agile as a monkey': Silver's actions are inhuman. I pointed out how much of the effect was achieved by alternative long and short sentences, and I revised formal work on capital letters and full stops.

I suggested that few human beings have been murdered with a crutch, and gave them a few minutes to think in silence about an unusual murder, and to work out how the story might be told. I should warn the reader that some serious over-writing follows:

> Mr Kaichi of the restaurant KAICHI DINER was agitated. One of his cooks was on strike, and his temper boiled. 'Why are you on strike?' he yelled. 'Not enough pay' answered the cook. Mr Kaichi dismissed him and went downstairs from his office to the public part of the restaurant. The cook was there. 'Work for me or you'll regret it!' yelled Mr Kaichi. 'You are being a fool!' 'Never! You are vile and evil and even smell a little!' said the cook.
>
> 'Then you give me no choice'. This was not Mr Kaichi's voice. No. It came from his mouth, but was different. It was deep, chocolaty and smooth. It sounded as though as soon as it came out of his mouth it melted.
>
> The cook ran. He leapt over table after table. As soon as he got to the glass door, Mr Kaichi acted. He grabbed a breadstick off a nearby table. He flung it with all his power. It rocketed through the air. It stuck itself snugly between the cook's shoulder blades. The cook choked. Mr Kaichi laughed. He laughed at murder! The cook was dead.
>
> (Rory 10)

For another example:

- Rory's equally over-written poem on p.189.

> A boy walked through Churchill graveyard. He could feel the icy wind blowing in his face. His eyes started to water. A tear fell on to the floor of the graveyard. Underground there were tiny tunnels which only your little finger could get through. Killer worms. Killer worms lived in those underground tunnels of the graveyard. Those killer worms heard that violent thud of the drop of water. They started to swim to the surface. The boy's tears kept on dripping down on to the ground. And the worms kept on swimming

up. When the worms got to the surface, they wrapped round the boy's legs. The boy fell. All the killer worms were slithering over his body. They swam into his mouth, they slithered up his nose, he could not breathe. There was blood oozing out of his body. He couldn't hear anything, feel anything, think of anything. He was dead.

(William 10)

A footnote to this story concerns a boy – I will call him Jack – who was almost stereotypically male in his passion for and ability in maths and science compared to his lack of interest, almost amounting, I felt sometimes, to a disdain for writing, especially poetry. I have not printed his work here, but his pen hardly came off the paper as he constructed a bloody and violent plot. The teacher and I were delighted to have the opportunity to send Jack around his (small) primary school so that he could show off a talent that no-one, least of all himself, believed he has until that morning.

• Ballads 'John Randall', etc., in Poetry.

The Old Sea-dog

Here is Stevenson again, introducing a character early on in the novel:

I remember him as if it were yesterday, as he came plodding to the inn door, his sea-chest following behind him in a hand-barrow; a tall, strong, heavy, nut-brown man; his tarry pigtail falling over the shoulders of his soiled blue coat; his hands ragged and scarred, with black, broken nails; and the sabre cut across one cheek, a dirty, livid white. I remember him looking around the cove and whistling to himself as he did so, and then breaking out in that old sea-song that he sang so often afterwards:

'Fifteen men on a dead man's chest –
Yo-ho-ho, and a bottle of rum!'

in the high old, tottering voice that seemed to have been tuned and broken at the capstan bars. Then he rapped on the door with a bit of stick . . . and . . . called roughly for a glass of rum. This, when it was brought to him, he drank slowly . . . lingering on the taste, and still looking about him at the cliffs and up at our signboard.

'This is a handy cove', says he, at length; ' and a pleasant sittyated grog-shop. Much company, mate?'

My father told him no, very little company . . .

'Well, then,' said he, 'this is the berth for me . . . I'll stay here a bit.'

I saw this as an opportunity to introduce another kind of rather extreme figure.

My pirate has a chirpy parrot with a broken wing. He has stitches on his whipped stomach because he was slashed with an electric whip! He also trots along on his sea legs. He sings a song. It goes 'Ho ho ho it's a pirate's life for me'. He admires his sea–chest every morning. In side there are 6 gleaming rubies, 10 shiny diamonds, 26 big crystals, and 8 delicate emeralds. He has a grand ship with 6 cannons and 3 trusty shipmates.

(Anon 10)

6

Biography: John Aubrey
Brief Lives

Ovall face. His eie a dark grey.

(John Aubrey)

Perhaps the sun liked Nanny

(10-year-old)

John Aubrey lived from 1626 to 1697. The quotation above comes from a book known as *Brief Lives*, which is a collection of biographical notes – anecdotes, really – about famous people. Some of the notes are very short, seven or eight lines; others, like the one on the poet John Milton, go on for pages. The book has a gossipy style which makes it inviting and unthreatening to this modern reader. I learn, for example, that 'Ben Johnson' (*sic* – that is, conventionally, 'Jonson') 'had one eie lower that t'other' and that Aubrey 'suppose[s]' that the death of the poet George Herbert at 36 was 'hastened' by his 'mariage'.

Aubrey provokes a short digression on linguistic correctness. It had to come into this book somewhere, and here it is. What are these: 'correct' spelling, punctuation and grammar? And what are these: 'conventional' spelling, punctuation and grammar? The first of these adjectives is of little use, and it begs a question: correct for whom? The second term makes dozens of arid conversations redundant. Aubrey's spelling in the passage quoted above and coming up in a longer extract later is not 'incorrect' even though it is, by modern standards, 'unconventional': a very different matter. I never write 'luv' when signing off, even to my most intimate friends, but I can't say it's incorrect: it is merely unconventional among people of my generation and, possibly, education.

Here are some examples of 'unconventional usage', some well-known, others less so. Underneath I have written the comments that would be made by a stickler for 'correctness' (a pedant):

'Who is in love with her? Who makes you their confident?'

'Their' should be 'his' or 'her', because the 'who' at the beginning is, presumably, singular.

That's Jane Austen, I think. Probably Mr Knightley to Emma in the novel *Emma*.

That was the most unkindest cut of all.

(William Shakespeare, Julius Caesar)

Either 'most' or '-est' is redundant. This should be either 'That was the most unkind cut of all' or, more likely, 'That was the unkindest cut of all'.

Take arms against a sea of troubles . . .

(William Shakespeare, Hamlet)

This is a mixed metaphor. The speaker begins with a military image, and moves to a nautical one.

These two are from Shakespeare, *Julius Caesar* and *Hamlet* respectively. The second is from 'To be or not to be', no less.

And specially to this congregation . . . that . . . they may hear . . .

(The Book of Common Prayer The Communion Service)

'they' should be singular – 'it' – because 'congregation' is a singular noun.

The True-Born Englishman

Wherever God erects a house of prayer,
The Devil always builds a chapel there
And 'twill be found, upon examination,
The latter has the largest congregation.

(Daniel Defoe)

'Largest' should be 'larger': the latter applies when the comparison is between two. Also, by modern standards, this verse is over-punctuated: at least, the comma at the end of the first line feels redundant.

> And they came over unto the other side of the sea
>
>   (Authorised Version, Mark 5:1)

> You should never begin a sentence with 'And'.
> 'The one [of two] you said it is the nicest'
>   (Dialogue from Hitchcock's *Shadow of a Doubt*, written, at least in part,
>   by the celebrated American playwright Thornton Wilder)

These examples suggest that 'rule' is an inappropriate word in language matters. And spelling only became regularised gradually in the decades following the publication of Samuel Johnson's *Dictionary* in 1755. Even today, we have alternative spellings of the same word: is it 'judgment' or 'judgement', for example; is it 'villainous' or 'villanous'. Language is constantly changing, and to insist on a legendary correctness is, however commonsensical it may seem, to insist that today's usage is the right one for all time. Later, on p.181 I am going to quote Chaucer. He calls 'April' 'Aprill', 'showers' 'shoures', 'sweet' 'soote' and 'drought' 'droghte'. Was he wrong? From what perspective would it be sensible to call him that?

On a calm day, it is possible to look at the sky and be sure that nothing up there is changing. But it is. Within half an hour, that cloud that looks like an elephant sucking with its trunk raised will look like a duck with its beak in the water. None of us reading a book and then, every now and then looking up, will perceive each change, but we know, without thinking about it, that the changes happen. The same is true of language. I owe this beautiful image to McWhorter (2001).

Split infinitives, for example, were forbidden when I was at grammar school. Indeed, the only benefit of a classical education (a colleague once said to me) was that she could spot the split infinitive in the preamble to 'Star Trek' on television: 'To boldly go where no man has gone before . . .' They are largely acceptable now. They were only forbidden by pedants because you simply can't split a Latin infinitive (*amare* – only one word, as all Latin infinitives are – or were) but you *can* split the English equivalent (*to love* – two words, as all English infinitives are).

Those who object to the modern use of 'hopefully' ('Hopefully it will be sunny') as opposed to its strictly adverbial use ('We went to the beach hopefully') do not, unaccountably, object to 'thankfully' being used in the same way ('Thankfully it didn't rain'). When the Olympics arrive, there will be letters to certain newspapers deploring the use of the sentence

'Great Britain medalled again today . . .' They will tell us that nouns should not be used as verbs. But these pedants express no objections to sentences like 'She *milk*ed the cow', 'I have just had my car *serviced*' or 'This window was *brick*ed up in the fifteenth century': all these are commonly accepted usages of nouns and verbs. Linguistic pedantry is an obsession of those who sense that it is easy to come across as superior if you understand a few questionable rules about a minority interest. To knowingly mock the sign 'five items or less' in Tesco gives you a claim to superiority.

We can see several examples of change in conventional grammar and spelling here in these lines from Aubrey: we would write 'as' rather than 'so'. We spell 'oval' and 'eye' differently, and we hardly recognise the word 'tuneable', though we can easily guess what it means. Here Aubrey describing the poet John Milton:

He was a spare man. He was scarce so tall as I am . . . middle stature.

He had abroun hayre. His complexion exceeding faire (he was so faire they called him the Lady of Christ's-college). Ovall face. His eie a darke grey.

Of a very cheerfull humour. He was very healthy, and free from all diseases, seldome took any Physique . . . He would be chearfull even in his Gowte-fitts: and sing.

He had a delicate tuneable Voice, and had good skill. His father instructed him. He had an Organ in his howse: he played on that most . . .

He had a very good memorie . . . His exercise was chiefly walking.

I wrote (using contemporary spelling, punctuation and grammar) about my best friend, who died in 2003:

He was round, and of small stature, no bigger than 5 foot 6. But his laughter was large, as large as his huge hospitality, as his friendship, as his unspoken wish you should have a good time in his house.

He always carried a camera, often two, and never let his friends part unless he had made them pose for photographs. Sometimes they liked this, sometimes they did not.

He kept in his house a small hand printing press, and with this he made little books of poems for his friends, who were, I believe, always grateful. He wrote poems, and sent them out, and many were published.

He was a great traveller, and every year, as well as visiting France, he would go to a country where he had never been before.

He had been a Royal Marine, and had some stories, mostly about mischief. He never told stories in which he had been a hero. He told me once that he had crashed a plane.

On his tombstone is written: 'O for a closer walk with Thee'. I chose that quotation, and I miss him every day.

I use sentences dotted all through Aubrey's book to help children to write chatty notes about someone they are fond of.

My nana loved sweet things, all fruits, but also boiled sweets and chocolate. She took two sugars in her tea.

She gave us biscuits from an old tin, and told us what each one was called. There were custard creams and jammy dodgers, I remember.

She lived on her own because my granddad died long ago, before I was born. We went to her house almost every week at least once.

She said 'If you stop biting your nails I will give you two bright pound pieces'.

She also loved the sun. When she died the weather was horrid. My mum said, 'Perhaps the sun liked Nanny'.

(Jill 10)

Then I was delighted to be asked to teach this passage to the 7- and 8-year-olds in my son Daniel's class. (Daniel is the teacher.) As I did so, I reflected that no-one had ever, almost certainly, taught John Aubrey to children, or even adolescents. A bundle of clichés dropped into my mental hallway: I was pushing the box, thinking outside the envelope, rolling out the trail, blazing the unthinkable . . . and doing all this alongside my son.

I have, somehow, to convey, without patronising, or even insulting, anyone, that these children are born with few privileges, at least as seen in the conventional sense. They do not go to a private school, for a start, and never will; neither do they go to the kind of state primary (often, but not always, linked to the Church of England) that works as a kind of substitute for many parents for a private school. This estate is not an easy place to walk around at night. And I was teaching them John Aubrey . . .

After I had read his words on Milton, I asked the children what they had remembered about them. It was almost everything Aubrey had written.

Often, they changed his words into their own, showing that they had not only remembered the passage and understood it, but had also made it part of their thinking. For example, one boy said that Milton 'never forgot things', which was his version of 'He had a very good memorie'. Then the children wrote:

> My best friend is Ellie. She is 4 years old and she is always playing with me and her favourite game is dolls and she always plays with my Hannah Montana house. She has blondey brown hair. She likes to eat strawberries. She likes to make snow angels in the snow. She has got a little brother called Lucas. She is always coming out with me. She has got a dog called Barney and she lives at number 11. She likes me going round hers . . .
>
> (Megan 7)

There were many pieces like this that showed Aubrey's influence. And then two little miracles happened. With the first, it is no wonder that the tenses are muddled, shifting between the present and the past. I had read my account of my friend John Cotton (to whose memory this book is dedicated) in case the Aubrey passage presented too many problems (which it hadn't). My ending had affected at least two children:

> My great granddad Tom died four days ago. He is 81 years old. He is short, he has wrinkles on his face. He used to give me things. He eats soup and noodles and drinks coffee. He lived in a care home. He was a nice great man. He had no hair, green eyes. I miss Granddad Tom very much.
>
> (Imogen 7)

> My cousin Rianna died. She had brown hair and she had curls. I used to go round hers and play with her and we used to go to the park and I used to push her on the baby swing and it was her birthday when she died. And her dolls are sweet and her cat was called Thomas.
>
> (Chanel 7)

Here, for the umpteenth time in my experience, I can see the therapeutic function that writing has. Chanel was in tears ten minutes after finishing this, and smiling and laughing at some poetry game ten minutes later. The act of writing helps us to reflect on what grieves us, and helps us to get it into a shape, so that we can less painfully, and, quite possibly, more purposefully, reflect on it.

A family feud is glimpsed in another piece of writing: 'My dad has a nanny but my granddad won't let me sleep at there'. Writing is, among other things, the place where we can help ourselves cope with the dark parts of our living.

7

Journals

When we were in the woods . . . we saw a few daffodils close to the water-side . . . but as we went along there were more and yet more and at last under the boughs of the trees, we saw that there was a long belt of them along the shore . . . I never saw daffodils so beautiful. They grew among the mossy stones about and about them; some rested their heads upon these stones as on a pillow for weariness and the rest tossed and reeled and danced and seemed as if they verily laughed with the wind that blew upon them over the lake.

(Dorothy Wordsworth *The Grasmere Journals* 15 April 1802)

Close observation is (or was) a cliché in progressive art education. Looking intensely at a leaf, a stone, a pebble, the spaces between the branches on winter trees; or at something mechanical, a throbbing car engine, or even something, on the face of it, boring, like the PE climbing apparatus – looking at all these things until (as Blake says, somewhere, that we should) it *hurts* . . . This was an activity much favoured in certain primary schools in the 1960s and 1970s.

There was a good reason. Such drawing educated the eye, the intellect and the hand, and thereby increased understanding of the object being observed and drawn. I often think of learning through close observation in terms of a triangle. The three-pointed relationship between the eye, the leaf (or stone, or pebble or whatever) and the hand with the pencil in it seems to me to be so potentially powerful.

And translate that into a genre of writing. There's the triangle between the eye (or ear, or tongue, come to that – you can taste words), the objects being observed (or heard, or tasted) and the hand that writes about it with a pencil. In that passage by Dorothy Wordsworth, the triangular relationship between her eye, the daffodils and her pencil is a powerful one. We can see this when she comes up with that phrase 'a long belt of them along the shore'; she captures both quietness and movement when she writes 'some rested their heads upon these stones as on a pillow for weariness and the rest tossed and reeled and danced . . .'

Both journal and sketchbook are underused tools in primary education. And because starting and developing this habit among children is a long term affair, and because I am rarely in a school more than three days in a year, I have been unable to collect children's writing. The reader will have to put up with a journal entry of my own:

I am in the Old Town of Prague. I have never been here before, and, more to the point, I have never been out of the British Isles so close to Christmas. It's been dark here for four hours, and it is cold, a hard cold, cold but very dry, no chance of rain or even snow. Children, heavy-coated, scarved and woolly-hatted, stand in rows on a temporary stage singing carols – most of the carols are sung in, I presume, Czech, but one is sung in English, and I am cheered to hear the children (none in school uniform) sing, with a big emphasis on the second syllable: 'Ve *vish* you a merry Christmas . . .'

Behind them the towers of the Tyn Church are like the towers you see in collections of fairy stories. Rapunzel's prince could have climbed up one of them. Earlier, I managed to get them in a shot with the other church in the square, St Nicholas, a more formal affair, where I got a thrill when I heard from a guide that 'Mozart played the organ here'. Stalls everywhere in the square sell roasted chestnuts, 50 kr. a bag; 'hot wine', 30 kr. 'grog' (this is rum mixed with hot water) 50 kr.; hot dogs; and sweet stuff that comes in rolls. I never checked this out.

All this is a long way emotionally from the Pinkus synagogue I visited this morning. There the walls are covered with the names of the Czech Jews who died in the concentration camp at Terezin, a few miles north of here. It is one thing to feel one's eyes fill with tears at sheer beauty (in Durham Cathedral, for example, or at a small harbour on a Greek island) and another to start to cry at unadulterated sadness, misery even.

I bought a reproduction of a drawing done by a child in that camp, and it is on my wall as I write. She has written 'Seder' ('Sabbath') over a drawing of a large family round a table, and someone has written her name in capitals: 'MEITNER, EVA'.

8

Beginnings

I mentioned in the introduction to this part of my book that children are all too often encouraged to begin stories with clichés (p.17). Here is a possible method of teaching children how to begin stories with, perhaps, vigour, or with a surprise, or at least with a fresh smell, rather than the stale smell of 'Once upon a time' or 'In a country long ago and faraway'. Because it has only just occurred to me, and I haven't, therefore, reflected on it much yet, let alone tried it, I haven't any examples of children's work.

When I am next in a school (which is after my deadline for this book) I will read them these sentences. Each opens a novel. Perhaps the reader would like to see which of them s/he can identify. I have cut out a name if it is a give-away:

A When I was four months old, my mother died suddenly and my father was left to look after me all by himself.
B When ___ _____ woke up on Monday morning, he found he was a girl.
C Sophie couldn't sleep.
D It was raining hard, but the sky was cloudless.
E If you went too near the edge of the chalk pit the ground would give way.
F The boy left home at first light, enough food and drink in his rucksack to last him the whole day.
G ____ was dead, to begin with.
H Butterflies live only short lives.
I When my parents split up, they didn't know what to do with me.

I will ask them to compare these openings with the story openings on p.16. I am sure that this will lead to discussion on questions about the differences between the two sets. Activities like this are often at their most educational when they are done in small groups of four or five children. In these occasions, the adults present – a learning support assistant, a parent, myself – circulate, jump-starting the occasional discussion that has stalled, nudging another in a new direction, making notes and generally being encouraging. I will ask children to think about:

A What are the three most important words in the sentence? Decide first which is the third most important, then the second most important, and finally the most important? As a group, discuss how the story might develop. Each member should write the next sentence, and the group compare what they have written.

B This is quite a shock to read in a first sentence. Imagine this boy who has just become a girl is about nine or ten, and the first thing he has to do is get ready for school. Then discuss the practical problems that will arise early in the school day. Discuss it all again as though the sentence read '. . . she found she was a boy'.

C is very short, but it opens possibilities. Talk in your group about things that have prevented you from sleeping. Why can't this girl sleep? What might happen next? Or what might have happened during the previous day?

D Another short opener: two clauses linked by a connective, with the shock in the last word. Each member of the group should write a similar sentence, where the last word provides a jolt. Then compare. The children could then swap sentences, and re-write them.

E This made me feel slightly nervous the first time I read it. Discuss why might that have been. What are the three most important words in this sentence? Where would you place 'if'? Write sentences beginning with 'If'. Compare; swap; re-write.

F In your group, discuss this. What genre is F written in? How do you know?

G Short. To the point. And the word 'dead' is in it! As a group, compose a sentence with no more that eight words in it, one of which must be 'dead'.

H This is a brilliant sentence. Imagine it with the word 'only' in different places: 'Butterflies only live short lives' or even 'Only butterflies live short lives'. Think about how important it is, where a writer places a word.

I If you've been a situation like this, carry on with the story. If you haven't . . . do it anyway.

I will ask the children to write sentences for stories that make the reader think, 'I'm going to read on . . . I want to know what is going to happen'.

The openings are from:

A Roald Dahl *Danny the Champion of the World*
  also C *The BFG*
B Anne Fine *Bill's New Frock*
D Carole Wilkinson *Dragon Keeper* and *Dragon Moon*
E Clive King *Stig of the Dump*
F Michael Morpurgo *Arthur High King of Britain*
G *A Christmas Carol*, of course
H Michael Morpurgo *The Butterfly Lion*
I Jacqueline Wilson *The Suitcase Kid*

9

Finally . . .

This section of my book is coming to an untidy end. As deadline approaches, I am aware of other writing ideas (despite its position, this is the last section I wrote) which I am sure will work with children – but I haven't had time to collect examples. For example, I often read the first chapter of Genesis to children, and suggest that they write their own stories about the beginnings of things. I link it up with creation stories from other traditions, which are available in Van Wolde 1996, and also:

- Rudyard Kipling's *Just So Stories*, especially 'How the Elephant Got His Nose' and

- Ted Hughes *How the Whale Became*.

Part II

Poetry

Introduction

'That's cool, that.'

(12-year-old)

1

I have been teaching poetry – mostly to primary school children, but also to secondary students, and sometimes to adults – ever since my first teaching practice more than four decades ago. Doing this has almost always, at some point, made me laugh inwardly (and sometimes outwardly) for simple happiness. Dylan Thomas said somewhere that poetry made his toenails twinkle. This phrase, twee as a Clinton birthday card for your 'nanna's ninetieth', is hard to bear, of course. But I know what he meant: there is in the reading of poetry (what he was talking about) and in the teaching of it (what I am writing about in this part of my book) a thrill that often manifests itself in physical ways. Some people report the hairs on the back of the neck being raised. Others report (I have never felt this, nor would I want to) 'my head being blown away'.

W.B. Yeats wrote, during his last years, about William Blake 'Who beat upon the wall / Till truth obeyed his call' ('An Acre of Grass', collected in 1984). Poetry, whether or not its readers are fully aware of it, is always dealing with truth; and dealing with truth will always be exciting, and in not altogether comfortable ways. So it may well raise hairs on the backs of necks; and for other, less timid, souls than mine, it might blow heads away. The children's experiences will rarely be as dramatic as 'beating upon the wall' (though sometime it will). But children are always alert both to truth in the large sense, and to the little truths that surround them. They fear the risk of misunderstanding any situation.

And finding truth . . . What else is the writing and study of poetry? Entertainers have for centuries used rhyme to entertain. Pam Ayres is their most prominent modern representative. But the comic monologue is the work of a comedian, which has much in common with that Clinton birthday card I mentioned earlier, and nothing in common with poetry.

One reason for the thrill that poetry often gives both its readers and its teachers is that it takes them deep into territory where truth cannot be avoided. You can't lie while praying, any more than you can steal the dinner money, rob a bank or wish your mother-in-law in her grave. You can't tell lies in a poem either: if you do, the poem will surely come to jagged pieces in your hands,[1] much as a prayer will do when you are trying to deceive yourself and the Almighty.

2

There have been, since the beginning of the last century and where we are in this one whenever you read this book, two ways of teaching poetry in primary schools. The first predominated until the 1960s: teachers taught pupils to appreciate poetry. This involved, mostly, learning poems by heart. I remember, in my last year at primary school, some time in the late 1950s, copying out the first three stanzas of Gray's 'Elegy in a Country Churchyard', and dying to tell the teacher that I already knew them because my mother had often recited them to me: 'The curfew tolls the knell of parting day, / The lowing herd wind slowly o'er the lea': these were, I now realise, the first iambic pentameters I internalised. Many older teachers have unpleasant memories of this practice.

Later, some time in the 1960s, teaching poetry became a matter of, not learning poetry, or learning about it (whatever that might mean) but of 'creative writing'. If it was strange that the first version of teaching poetry rarely, if ever, led to the children's *writing* poetry, it was even stranger that the latter almost never involved the children *reading* it. This change was part of a wider political movement, a pseudo-democracy that was a dictatorship of, not so much of the proletariat, but of feelings.

However callow they are, they are valid in a poem. It's expressed in the mantra 'everyone's opinion was worth as much as anyone else's'. The study of white dead males who were, by and large, the poets a previous generation had been asked to learn by heart, or by rote, were now less important than giving children opportunities to 'express themselves'.

In fact, the 'progressive movement' had a far weaker grip on schools than the media suggested. Almost all teachers travelled on down the same chalk-and-talk road as before, as if 'child-centred education' had never been invented. Few teachers asked questions like, what else could education be but child-centred?

But where progressive education did take hold, it sometimes meant that a child's expression of her feelings overrode any discussion of craft: only sincerity counted. Indeed, when I started teaching creative writing on my first teaching practice in 1965, I never connected the children's writing to the tradition: Shakespeare, say, or Christina Rossetti. When I did read poems to the children, it was always outside the 'creative writing' lesson. Poems came as entertainment at the end of the day, and they were always modern poems. I offered no sense of what the tradition might be.

I saw the fruit of this sentimental belief – that poetry is simply self-expression – many years later when a head teacher, who was of an age with the children I had taught in the 1960s, told me that he wrote poetry. I said what I always say on these occasions – they are frequent – 'And who do you read?' He replied: 'I never read poetry, I don't want anything I read to affect my work'. As far as he was concerned, all that mattered was his feelings, and getting them down on paper. As far as I am concerned, he may as well have been a guitarist who had never heard Segovia, John Williams or Eric Clapton.

In this part of my book, my aim is to bring the teaching of traditional poetry and the teaching of creative writing together.

– – –

Here's a memory of inward laughter and someone becoming, if only for a moment, a brother in the mystery. About ten years ago, I talked to over a hundred 13-year-olds at a local comprehensive school. (This was a very cost-conscious school, and class-sized groups were, it had been made clear, out of the question). I made notes about this session as soon as I got home. They were something like this, though I am polishing a little as I type:

As a primary school teacher, I am used to children sitting on the floor, where I often sit with them. These students, though, are too old to sit on the floor. But they are, at least in part, still children to me: my son is the same age. They are arranged in a rough semi-circle on wooden chairs on a wooden floor, and the scraping and banging grumbles through the period, five or ten minutes, as they file in. I wait nervously. Once they have dumped their gear – bags and anoraks – and (kind of) settled, it seems to me that the most acne-ridden, the most spiky-haired, the most testosterone-fuelled males are sitting in the front row. Their legs are spread wide like the legs of pundits on 'Match of the Day': 'Impress us' they are saying with their body language: not just their legs, but their eyes, and their arms folded protectively across their chests. 'Impress us . . .'

With no introduction, nervously, but with the kind of courage that the experience of poetry has given to me hundreds of times, I recite these lines. They were written by a Victorian Anglo-Catholic spinster, Christina Rossetti, whose brother, Dante Gabriel, was something like the Damien Hurst of his time (though, heaven knows, the poet was no Tracy Emin):

> What are hard? Sea sand and sorrow.
> What are frail? Spring blossoms and youth.
> What are brief? Today and tomorrow.
> What are deep? The ocean and truth.

(Christina Rossetti 1904)

For similar poems:

- Charles Causley's poems 'What has happened to Lulu', 'Who?' and 'Why?', all in *Collected Poems for Children* are modern examples of poems composed almost entirely of questions to which children respond. Another example is Ted Hughes' 'Leaves' in his *Collected Poems for Children*, which is a descendant of the old rhyme 'Who killed Cock Robin?'

I stop. That is the whole poem. Silence. And a boy in the front row says, not just to me, and not really to anyone else, really, not to his teachers, not to his peers, not looking behind him, not looking along his row, not changing his posture one bit, his legs still parted, his arms still folded across his chest . . . he says to the silence in the room, a silence brought about by a Victorian poet and me:

'That's cool, that'.

That excited me. The memory still does. That upped my heartbeat. Introducing Christina Rossetti to a large class of comprehensive students on an estate in Ipswich was wonderful, but being paid a compliment far more significant than any compliment (and, surprisingly perhaps, there have been a few) that Ofsted could pay me was even better.

It was exciting because it confirmed what I already knew, deep in my heart: that a Victorian Anglo-Catholic spinster poet, born 1830, died 1894, could cut the mustard in the twenty-first century in a school the like of which she couldn't have imagined. I try to work out why. There are eight statements in the poem. Sea sand is hard; sorrow is hard. Spring blossoms are frail; youth is frail. Today is brief; tomorrow is brief. The ocean is deep; and truth is deep. Some are truths about concrete nouns, some about abstract nouns (this leads to interesting discussion about grammar, as so much poetry does). The rhythms are as simple as the rhymes in a nursery rhyme; but paradoxically, the poem is profound; and, unlike a nursery rhyme, the whole thing is solemn. The line about the frailty of youth will strike a chord at some level or other with all teenagers.

Here is another example of shared excitement. A week before I drafted this, I read to a group of children Thomas Hardy's 'To the Moon' (see p.172). One of the children, Anya (10) wrote this, her first stanza of five:

'What have you dreampt of distant star
Oh, so far
Lying still, in the dark?'
'I have dreampt of many things,
Pegasus flying with fragile wings . . .'

It is not easy to decide now which gives me the greatest thrill: Hardy's characteristic poem, which I have read more than a hundred times, often on my own, but often with children; or Anya's writing, a speck of dust to Hardy's star, of course, but something crafted in his presence. And therefore a kind of miracle: I have taught alongside Thomas Hardy, as I had taught in that comprehensive school alongside Christina Rossetti. And there is that line, where Anya has brought in learning from other lessons.

The thrill that I have been writing about is not chiefly about the children's poems, but about the interaction between, on the one hand, poetry by Rossetti and Hardy, and on the other, the children's progress in listening, thinking and writing. That interaction, in both listening and writing, helps children in their exploration of their own natures, the nature of the world around them, the relationship between themselves and (crucially) their language. It is always the learning that matters.

There must be no sentimentality about children's writing. I'm uneasy when teachers approach me and say: 'I've got these wonderful poems my children have written . . .' Indeed, I back away, if not physically, at least inside my head. Children, I would say, had I the courage, have had intense experience; but it is limited; they have but a tiny grasp of the craft, let alone the technique, required to make what their teachers and their parents call 'wonderful poems'. 'Your children', I want to say, 'have not written "wonderful" poems'.

On the other hand, children have in their grasp what all but very few adults lack: a raw honesty, courage about what they write. They have a willingness (unlike that head teacher I cited on p.73) to listen to the examples of those who have written poems before they existed. And they also have a willingness to play with, taste and experiment with words. As educators, it is our job to help them build on these things: to help them retain as long as possible that honesty, and that willingness to play. It is our job to teach them craft and technique. And the main argument of this section of my book is that it is our job to introduce them to the work of great poets, knowing that those poets will help them learn.

But it is not our job, whether we are parents or teachers, to talk about children as though they are the next Sappho, the next Homer, the next Shakespeare, where the word 'wonderful', though rather vague, becomes, at least, relevant. It is our job to help children to tell the truth through the medium of poetry. And that is a job that concerns right and wrong.

I know how extravagant, how romantic, how sentimental those sentences about teaching alongside Thomas Hardy and Christina Rossetti may sound to some. But I hope to show that, when I summon writers into classrooms, they teach, or their ghosts teach, alongside me. I have already written a book (1999) which was composed in part of poems written by children in the ghostly presence of Shakespeare. Now, here come, in no particular order, the authors of Ecclesiastes and Proverbs in the Old Testament of the Bible; Geoffrey Chaucer; the anonymous makers of nursery rhymes, ballads and epitaphs; Alexander Pope; John Clare; Thomas Hood; Christina Rossetti; Sara and Mary Coleridge; Thomas Lovell Beddoes; Gerard Hopkins . . . and others.

3

Four difficulties

> 'As to poetry, you know', said Humpty Dumpty, stretching out one of his great hands, '*I* can repeat poetry as well as other folk if it comes to that—'
>
> 'Oh, it needn't come to that!' Alice hastily said . . .
>
> (*Through the Looking Glass*)

There are four serious difficulties that assail the teaching of poetry to children. The first is obvious: very few people, and therefore, by extension, very few teachers, enjoy it. Some even fear it: an education officer with whom I had very good professional relations once backed away from me, palms raised outwards, when I mentioned the word 'poetry'. He would have raised garlic had any been about his person, as though I were a werewolf. He would have shown the panic about to grip Alice in the passage above.[2] Poetry is seen by many who have never read much as something limp and unuseful, 'a skirt thing, a church thing' as an American writer once put it; something an effete young man might dabble with when he has too much inherited wealth and not enough responsibility and sense. Even today, the words 'poet', 'young man', 'starving' (he's gambled away all that inherited money) and 'garret' fly automatically together in people's minds. Millais' painting of that 'wonderful boy', Thomas Chatterton, lying dead on his bed in his upper room, is too much part of the social definition of what a poet is.

Many people – probably most – dislike the very idea of poetry in the same way that they dislike people whom they think are pretentious, whom they see as too keen to impress; whom they see as over-earnest. They suspect, these poetry-haters, that poetry is all about eternal truths, and they know that eternal truths are not for them, thanks very much. Certainly, poetry is called, sometimes, to speak for a nation that has lost thousands of her young men, and to say in Binyon's words:

> With proud thanksgiving, a mother for her children,
> England mourns for her dead across the sea . . .[3]
>
> (collected in Gardner 1972)

And I know many poetry-haters who, in the windswept autumnal park in front of the war memorial, are moved by those lines every November.

And if poetry wasn't called to say these words, who else would? Politicians? Newspaper reporters? That slick person on television with the less than winning smile? Someone has to say it. I'd trust a poet.

But poetry is also called to say things like this:

Julius Caesar Pompey Green
Wore a jacket of velveteen . . .

which may not be about an ultimate truth, but is about the debunking strand that all human beings have inside them, unless they have no sense of humour, especially about their elders and betters. Julius Caesar? Who's he?

The second difficulty is: some teachers try to teach the writing of poetry to children without ever giving them the experience of poems. This is a direct descendant of the poetry-teaching strategies I've described in pp.00 above. It's like teaching photography when you've never seen a photograph to someone else who hasn't seen one.

And the third difficulty is related. The examples that are often read to children are no more than bad jokes. Indeed, unfortunately, these jokes form the larger part of much of the 'poetry' that is published. If you look at the poetry shelf in the children's section of your local Waterstones, sparse as it will be, you will see, among the handsome, tubby Macmillan anthologies, the Collecteds of a few giants (Causley, Hughes) and some noble but unadventurous anthologies . . . you will find skinny volumes with the words 'underpants', 'potty', 'bum', 'knickers' etc. on the spines. The message that these books send to children is that any funny rhyme is a poem, and also (and therefore) that any poem must be funny.

Spike Milligan was a comic genius. But he is not a good influence. I have reviewed many books with rhymes that he would have winced at: 'If you grab a pig / And hold it by its snout / You can use its tail / To pull a wine cork out.' The dumpers of this kind of rubbish on the bookshelves of Waterstones and, more seriously, on the shelves of school libraries, do not understand that this kind of verse can be done, and is well done, in the playground, and has been done, for generations. From something like forty years ago comes:

I'm a little girl guide dressed in blue
And here are the things that I must do:

Be nice to the teacher, curtsey to the queen
And show my knickers to the football team.

and

Hurrah hurrah I've lost me bra
And me pants are in me boyfriend's car

And here's a 5-year-old boy in the school where I had my first attempt at headship in the early 1980s. It was our custom to have a sharing assembly every Friday afternoon. The teachers had planned everything. This boy, who had been almost completely silent during his first week at school, must have wondered what was going on. He'd have clocked that children are going to the front and saying things they are proud of. Then, he stood up in front of everyone at the end of his first week and said:

Potatoes and gravy
Potatoes and gravy
That's the stuff you get in the Navy
I'm happy by gum
When I'm tight as a drum
Filled up with potatoes and gravy.

All of these rhymes have a humour, a vigour, an honesty and even a tradition (where had that boy got his rhyme from? A retired sailor-grandad?) that none of those adult-written books have, full as they are of potties, bums, pimples, bogies and knickers.

Even when the poems in the children's book section of the local library, or the local Waterstone's, aren't jokes, they are often 'contemporary' and 'relevant', poems that 'reflect children's experience'. But, as any serious adult reader of poetry knows, poems must do much more that this. They must extend us, surprise us and even, quite often, bewilder us. I didn't expect the secondary students listening to Rossetti's poem (p.74 above) to understand it at one hearing, any more than I did at my first reading. But the boy's comment, 'That's cool', showed, first, that poetry scores before it is fully understood, and second, that there is 'relevance' where you least expect it.

The fourth difficulty hardly needs spelling out. We live at a time when the market culture has forced our elders and betters to look askance on anything that doesn't lead to financial benefit. Any activity that isn't 'cost-effective' is worthless. Mrs Thatcher (as she then was) tried to convince us that it was a market-oriented society that had permitted the existence of the Good Samaritan to be rich enough to help a fallen man. Some of us believed that the point of the parable (St Luke 10: 25–37) was that a member of a despised race was more capable of mercy than a priestly member of a respected race.

What followed then – in governments of both colours, of course – was the assumption that everything good will follow the market's demands. Meanwhile, teachers concerned with the arts fought – and still have to fight – for time and resources. While this is obviously true of the visual arts and drama and music, which both require resources of space and equipment – violins, guitars, paint, clay, rooms to work in, studios, theatres – it is also true of the 'cheap' business of writing. Teachers can find no time for re-drafting; and indeed, I was working under so much pressure of time when I wrote this book – not from my publisher, but from schools – that I have not been able to let the children redraft nearly as much as I would have liked.

So, the fourth problem is that the task of helping children towards the truth is scuppered by the mechanics of school life as dominated by philistine government policies. The predominant need is to put professional weight behind making sure the school is near the top of the league tables. All this apparatus damages children. They often spend weeks preparing for SATs. Their PE and Art lessons are in many schools cancelled. And then they are distressed in exam situations. The ambience surrounding teachers and children is profoundly philistine. But, as we all know, that is the way things are going, and there is an increasing recklessness about it. Publishers have acute antennae when it comes to the way the wind is blowing in education, and a representative of the main publisher of poetry for children in the UK recently told a distressed gaggle of its poets that, because of poetry's low priority in the National Curriculum, she did not want to receive any more manuscripts. That says much about poetry and the search for truth in relation to more National Curriculum-friendly subjects.

The voice of anonymous: poems from the oral tradition

1

How many blackberries grow in the sea? Nonsense verse, and children writing it

I answered him honest, I answered him true,
Of men there are many, of trees there are few.

(10-year-old)

The passage that Samuel Foote wrote to test Charles Macklin's memory (p.21) led to some lively verbal clowning by some children, but nonsense verse is a surer bet – see the example above. Every language, I hope, has a tradition of this kind of material. English has, pre-eminently, Edward Lear and Lewis Carroll. There will be more of Carroll later, though nothing of Lear, who, with his Tonghy-Bonghy-Bo, his Quangle-Wangle, his toe-less Pobble, and his Dong with his worrying and (some say) Freudianly significant luminous nose, has entranced a few children in every generation, and almost as certainly bored many more to tears. Either way, his owl and his pussycat have sailed in my imagination for most of my life. I remember, as a child, hoping that their marriage (symbolised, of course, by a ring that had previously adorned a Piggy-wig's snotty nose, and performed by a turkey who lived, rather isolated, one might have thought, for an Anglican cleric, on the hill) was a happy one.

But there is an oral tradition in English, and that is what this part of my book celebrates and uses in its mission to help children learn more about their language. But first a glimpse of nonsense from Scottish-English, and then glimpses from two other languages. Here's Anonymous playing word games:

Hokey pokey winky wum
How do you like your taties done?
Snip snap snorum hi popalorum
Kate go scratch it
You are out!

Am stram gram
Pic et pic et colegram
Bour et bour et ratatam
Am stram gram!

Annchen dannchen
Diddchen daddchen
Evarde bewerde
Bittehende battchen
Evarde bewerde bu
Ab bist du!

All three are counting-out rhymes: four or five children stand in a line, and another counts along it, chanting the words and emphasising the beat (*HOkey POkey WINKey WUM*) until (*Out! Gram! Du!*) someone is out. The process is repeated until there remains a winner. The second and third rhymes are French and German respectively (Haughton 1988).

We can hear the voice of the world's childhood tribe here, and it is evidence of a common humanity more certain than any other, because everyone has been a member of it once. Most of us now can only 'eaves-drop all [their] talk / With an amused look' (to quote R.S. Thomas' lovely poem 'Children's Song' 1993). But the wisest of us know that of such is the Kingdom of Heaven, and that once you can draw like Raphael or write like Dante, you must spend what time you have left learning to draw or write like a child.

You can hear the tribe's most benign noises all over the world outside school playgrounds at what the Americans call 'recess' and we call 'play-time': the songs, the rhythms, the skipping rhymes, the counting-out rhymes. I have been collecting these verses for decades, sometimes with the help of the Opies (1955, 1959, 1988) and sometimes under my own steam, and I say the older and more obscure examples to children, and ask them to write new ones in an unheard-of language, or to write some in their own language in the grip of the obvious metre that I've demonstrated.

These children are aged between four and six. Some went for simplicity. Here are two anonymous examples by 5-year-olds:

One egg round
One egg fat
One egg triangle
One egg cracked
OUT

Star moon
Star moon
Sun rain
Sun rain
Drip drop
You're out

But then something odd happened. Most of the children forgot about the counting-out aspect of the exercise, and simply wrote nonsense. One four-year-old, who had been at school three weeks, dictated this to her teacher:

Higgledy piggledy cauliflower and cheese
I want a slice of ham with it please.
Higgledy piggledy cauliflower and cheese
I want ten olives with it please.
Higgledy piggledy cauliflower and cheese
I can't eat all this mummy please.
Higgledy piggledy cauliflower and cheese
I have room for ice cream please.

(Grace 4 (though, as she said, nearly 5))

This is not, of course, completely nonsensical at all. Easily visible inside it is what must be the infuriating rule imposed on the tribe that you may have ice cream, but only when you have finished your cauliflower and cheese.

> Blonde hair brown hair black hair here
> Has anybody seen
> My lost ear?
> Is it in the park or the field or the classroom?
> No my dear
> Is it in the grass or in a box?
> Help me find my ear
> Have you found my ear
> No
> Have you found my ear
> Yes it's right here.

(Maud 6)

We turn the corner here from verse into poetry. For the first time in this section, here is material that makes it certain that sometimes Anonymous is the real thing, a poet. Read this piece, if possible, as though you have never read it before:

The Man in the Wilderness

The Man in the Wilderness asked of me
'How many blackberries grow in the sea?'
I answered him as I thought good,
'As many red herrings grow in the wood'.

The Man in the Wilderness asked me why
His hen could swim and his pig could fly.
I answered him briskly as I thought best,
'Because they were born in a cuckoo's nest'.

The Man in the Wilderness asked me to tell
The sands in the sea, and I counted them well.
Says he with a grin, 'And not one more?'
I answered him bravely, 'You go and make sure'.

(Eighteenth century)

I enjoy the way Anonymous brings out two characters. The first, like a teasing teacher, the Man in the Wilderness, asks impossible questions; but the second, a far more interesting person, answers 'briskly' and 'bravely' and as she 'thought good'. I always imagine this second person as a pert, intelligent female, rather like Elizabeth Bennet in *Pride and Prejudice*. She stands up for herself. The madness of the other lines in the poem – the blackberries growing in the sea, the herrings in the wood, the swimming hen and the flying pig – all this tends to hide the presence of these two people.

In another version, the irregular verbs have been made regular. Has it come from a child? I have often noticed how often children change, for example, 'swum' into 'swimmed', as here:

The Man in the Wilderness asked of me
How many red strawberries growed in the sea?
I answered him again as best I could,
As many red herrings as swimmed in the wood.

I read the first version to a group of children who had been labelled (though not by me) 'gifted writers'. I explained, briefly, the meaning of 'oral tradition'. Poems come to us without, at first, having been written down. They come by word of mouth, father to son, mother to son, father to daughter, mother to daughter, much as family stories do. I did the only glossing necessary ('tell' in line 9, which modern English has in 'tally' = 'count'), and I talked about how each line was a nonsense that helped the poem to become an even bigger nonsense; and then we played with the insistent metre.

I asked the children to come up with mysterious figures to replace 'the man in the wilderness', and we brainstormed a few. Then the children wrote:

The girl at the seashore asked me why
The sky touched the sea and the sea touched the sky.
I replied with a smile 'Try looking again,
At the far horizon and the world of men'.

The girl at the seashore questioned me,
Could I fetch a star from the depths of the sea?

I looked quite hard, and proudly replied,
'There's a starfish, you know', and then I sighed.

The girl at the seashore asked me if
The world would go slow and then go stiff.
I answered sadly with a little shame
'If it does, it's humans you need to blame'.

(Niamh 10)

The hag in the desert asked me why
Pencils could write but couldn't fly.
I answered her with an answer quite truthful.
'There're already being used as something useful'.

The hag in the desert asked Oh when
Ants would be as tall as men.
I answered her with an answer quite deadly
'They are the perfect size already'.

(Giles 10)

The children seemed more than able to set off jogging with an imitation of the original's metre (Di-dum-di-di-dum-di-dum-di-dum) but, in later lines, when the meaning of what they were writing, nonsense or not, began to take precedence in their minds, the business of juggling accented and unaccented syllables proved more difficult. So I helped, I hope. For example, 'I replied with a smile "Try looking again, / At the far horizon and the world of men"' may not be perfect, but it is better than the original, which had read 'I replied with a smile – "try to look again / Look far in the horizon to the world of men"'.

Rhyme was a different matter: the dodgy couplings 'truthful/useful' and 'deadly/already' simply do not matter in work of this kind because they are a feature of the oral tradition the children are using anyway. They have, therefore, a kind of authenticity. I remember being mildly indignant when I was a child at the rhymes 'lemons / St Clements', 'farthing / St Martin's' and so on in the famous cockney rhyme about London churches, as well as the 'puddle / middle' in that rhyme about Doctor Foster, and the tree's 'top' in 'Hush-a-bye baby' that rhymes with 'rock'. And the pail of 'water' that is supposed to rhyme with 'after' in

'Jack and Jill' suggests that someone in the oral tradition chain is more interested in Jill's 'tumbling' than in technical accuracy. As, indeed, I am.

But more important than these technical issues is the fact that sometimes the poems seemed to approach something profound, even troubling. They touch, it seems to me, on myth. By this word I do not mean 'untruth', as modern usage suggests ('your story about the dog eating your homework is a myth'), but a story that is an attempt to shed a light on some aspect of the human situation. In some of these lines, there is the modern myth about the conservation of our rivers, our air, our words and forest, a myth that resonates powerfully for our children. For example, one girl, Ellie, aged 9, wrote the following for her second stanza of three. It is crying out for a one-syllable adjective before 'cage' in the first line (you can see what I mean with my suggestions), but there we are:

> The man in the [blue, green, hard, soft] cage asked me why
> A tree should live and he should die.
> I answered him honestly, I answered him true,
> Of men there are many, of trees there are few.

I find I can forgive any roughness in the first couplet once I've arrived at the end of the second! But I wish now, as I type this up, that I'd suggested to Ellie that she might be more casual with her grammar, and use her ear more carefully, and change 'honestly' in the third line to 'honest'. Why can't 'honest' act as an adverb? 'Answer', later in the line is a noun acting as a verb . . . It's a common practice in English. And that alteration makes – or would have made – a lovely couplet:

> I answered him honest, I answered him true,
> Of men there are many, of trees there are few.

And if we'd found that one-syllable adjective for the first line, we'd have arrived at:

> The man in the bright cage asked me why
> A tree should live and he should die.
> I answered him honest, I answered him true,
> Of men there are many, of trees there are few.

The 'girl at the seashore' in Naimh's poems has a mythical feel as well. Is she a mermaid? In that line about 'the horizon and the world of men', Niamh's writing hints at anxieties she feels about growing up. That issue often arises in children's writing. It is another myth, and its force is increased in our times by the understandable obsession society has about children's safety. The 'hag in the desert' that has wandered into Giles' mind also seems disturbingly familiar. Strange figures who demand answers of a lonely traveller, or who insist on telling stories to that figure, feature widely in our culture. Think of the Ancient Mariner, for example. And there's Meet-on-the-Road, coming later on pp.107–8.

I was working with a class of 7- and 8-year olds. They hadn't been label-led as 'gifted' or 'keen', and they didn't get as far as making complete poems, or even stanzas, but they did come up with some resonant lines. It is less easy here to see evidence of myth. In making these lines, the children are simply ducking under, or leaping over, the hurdle of common sense: a vital activity for anyone who wants to reach the nerves of his or her writing:

Why do my shows talk to my orange?
Why is James' jumper made out of blood?
How many crocodiles drop from the sky?
Why does Mrs Hall dance on the matchbox?
Why are cats and dogs made from custard?

But when I asked the children to think of some people to take the place of the man in the wilderness, the myths arose, as they thought of, among others, 'the ghost at the door', 'the singer at the seaside' and 'the skeleton at the garage'. Through nonsense ('How many red strawberries growed in the sea?') you come to the kind of truth that is embedded in myth: 'it's humans you need to blame', for example. And 'of men there are many, of trees there are few'. Here is a myth that children are acquainted with, the one about our responsibility for the world, and the need to act it out in responsible use of the world's resources.

I use this next poem to round off writing lessons based on the above. I haven't used it to stimulate writing: sometimes poetry is there just to delight. Children love the sad dying fall at the end of each stanza. Sometime I point out that this has been achieved in a clever way: the first couplet rhymes, so something in our ear expects the second one to rhyme as well. But it doesn't and, what's more, it ends very downbeat: 'crying'. While some adults tell me that this is 'pulling a poem apart' and thereby 'destroying it', children don't feel this, and enjoy it as much as I do.

I gave my love a cherry without a stone;
I gave my love a chicken without a bone;
I gave my love a ring without an end;
I gave my love a baby with no crying.

How can there be a cherry without a stone?
How can there be a chicken without a bone?
How can there be a ring without an end?
How can there be a baby with no crying?

A cherry when it's blooming, it has no stone;
A chicken when it's piping, it has no bone;
A ring, when it's rolling, it has no end;
A baby when it's sleeping has no crying.

- - -

I wanted experience with more nonsense poems. I found this one in Christopher Ricks' *Oxford Book of English Verse*. Its anonymous composer is probably from the eighteenth century:

I saw a fishpond all on fire
I saw a house bow to a squire
I saw a parson twelve feet high
I saw a cottage near the sky
I saw a balloon made of lead
I saw a coffin drop down dead
I saw two sparrows run a race
I saw two horses making lace
I saw a girl just like a cat
I saw a kitten wear a hat
I saw a man who saw these too
And said though strange they all were true.

I read this poem to a group of 8-year-olds — not labelled as 'keen writers', but keen enough in their way — in a village on the outskirts of the city of

Durham. Once again, I explained the notion of 'oral tradition' and I asked, 'Any comments? What about that poem? Any adjectives for it?'

Someone said 'It rhymed'. I waited: a lot of effective question-and-answer time consists of the teacher's waiting. There's thinking going on in silences, and often we are impatient, and foreclose on the children's learning by giving them answers that they would be better off moving towards themselves. Then someone said 'It's awkward'. I suppose that my expression said something like 'Yessss . . . and . . .?' And then, almost immediately, another child said: 'It's nonsense', and another 'It's silly'.

Well, yes it is, of course. But then I said it like this:

all on fire I saw a house
bow to a squire I saw a parson
twelve feet high I saw a cottage
near the sky I saw a balloon
made of lead I saw a coffin
drop down dead I saw two sparrows
run a race I saw two horses
making lace I saw a girl
just like a cat I saw a kitten
wear a hat I saw a man who saw these too
and said though strange they all were true.

This poem, arranged like this, offers images of life two or three centuries before the children's own. There's that parson, aware of his relatively lowly station in the village, who bows to a squire, and that girl who sits making lace. Houses burnt more readily then, of course, because they were made of wood, and lead coffins were an all too familiar sight, even for children. And, of course, infant mortality being as high as it was, many of the coffins were small.

Read like this, of course, the poem isn't nonsense. I asked the children to make up sentences, and write them down like this, going up a step after the noun. Note that technical term:[1] I had already signalled 'adjectives' in my earlier questions. In this way, children come across these words, not in a context-free 'List of some interesting adjectives', but where they work, where they count. They have to do this without any intention of making a joke:

                           Jump over a gate

I saw a dog
Then more:

                           Pulling a cracker

I saw a party-goer

                           With his hands in the sink

I saw a husband

                           Dancing to hip hop

I saw my brother

                           Saying his prayers

I saw the priest

                           Burning the rubbish

I saw a fire

                           Flying to Mars

I saw a rocket

                           Coming out at last

I saw the honeysuckle

Then they put a ring round the last part ('I saw the honeysuckle'), and put an arrow swooping it up into the gap before the first, 'Jump over a gate' and they get, of course:

I saw the honeysuckle Jump over a gate

Then they carry on down, matching the two halves of each sentence as they have appeared.

I saw a dog Pulling a cracker
I saw a party-goer With his hands in the sink
I saw a husband Dancing to hip hop
I saw my brother Saying his prayers
I saw the priest Burning the rubbish
I saw a fire Flying to Mars
I saw a rocket Coming out at last

This exercise produces, to say the least, pleasing images. But some of the images have a surrealist feel, such as that fire flying to Mars. And others are potentially subversive: what rubbish is that priest burning? Modern writers

– these children – are hacking into the oral tradition, and that experience links them to their forerunners in the childhood tribe, who could neither read nor write at all. Much as a worshipper or a tourist in a medieval cathedral is in touch with worshippers from seven centuries ago, these children are in touch with their distant ancestors.

If the children arrange themselves in pairs, and you ask them to write verse with joint authorship, this offers a good opportunity for oral work. If you eavesdrop on their conversations, you will hear much animated discussion, much intense negotiation of lines. I insist that they do not compose their lines with half an eye on the resulting bizarre images. The more ordinary their original sentences are, the funnier the final result:

> I saw a river learning French
> I saw a man fall off a shelf
> I saw books melting in the sun
> I saw an ice cream snapping in the water
> I saw a crocodile eating a fly
> I saw a frog whooshing down the road
> I saw a fire engine hopping at the farm
> I saw a rabbit flood at Durham Cathedral
>
> (Ben and Kieran 8)

The children had just finished a term when they had been studying Henry VIII, and that study (or the evidence of it on the walls) influenced their writing, producing at least one pleasingly bizarre line:

> I saw a horse flapping in the breeze
> I saw a blind barking at the door
> I saw a dog marry Anne Boleyn
> I saw Henry VIII shopping in Tesco
> I saw Mr Sedgwick explode with a bang
> I saw a balloon being posted through my door
> I saw an envelope disappear in the sky
> I saw the sun jumping over a fence
>
> (Beth and Becky 8)

Another way to make a nonsense poem is to mix the senses, as in this poem:

My name is hunky-Dory Daly.
   I ride the weather out.
I see the thunder through the trees
   and hear the lightning shout.

I'm gifted with these useless gifts:
   to smell the bright snowfall,
to taste spring rain on a winter day
   and the cuckoo's call.

My name is hunky-Dory Daly.
   My gifts I'll give to you
if you will ride the storm with me
   and see the weather through.

                                 (FS)

Children do this readily. The technique – mixing the senses – has a name: synaesthesia.

Other nonsense poems:

- Charles Causley 'Old Mrs Thing-um-e-bob', *Collected Poems for Children*

- Stevie Smith 'My Cats' in *Collected Poems*.

- The following poems by Christian Morgenstern, by various translators: 'The Knee', 'The Two Roots' and 'The Sniffle', all in *Junior Voices the Second Book*; 'The Snail's Monologue', 'The Experiment', 'Korf's Joke' and 'The Fence' all in *Junior Voices the Third Book*; 'The Names of the Months' and 'The Dreamer' in *Junior Voices the Fourth Book*.

- Hugh Haughton's anthology *The Chatto Book of Nonsense Poetry*. This book has long been out of print, but it is worth snapping up if you see it on Amazon or in a second-hand bookshop.

- Kit Wright 'Nutter' and 'If you're no good at cooking', 'Song Sung by a Man on a Barge to Another Man on a Different Barge in Order to Drive him Mad' and other poems (*The Magic Box*)

- *Verse and Worse* by Arnold Silcock contains much semi-nonsense verse.

- *The Hat* Carol Ann Duffy

- Shel Silverstein *Where the Sidewalk Ends* and *A Light in the Attic*

- John Agard *I Din Do Nuttin*, London Puffin, *Say it Again Granny* and *Laughter is Egg*

Many of the poems in these books are nonsense that (like much of the best of this genre) is not altogether nonsense.

2

Anonymous speaks again: nursery rhymes and other folk poetry

There are three twentieth-century Oxford anthologies covering the whole of English poetry since. The first was published in 1900, the second in 1972, and the most recent in 1999. One striking change, for our purposes, is that nursery rhymes were ignored in 1900 and 1972, but recognised by the editor Christopher Ricks in 1999 for what they surely are: poems.

I have written earlier (pp.77–78) about teachers who find poetry too difficult and earnest; who feel that they have to hoick their emotions up to an unaccustomed level to get close to understanding it, let alone teaching it. Well, it is like that sometimes, of course. But what about the sheer pleasure to be had from the rhythms, enhanced by repetition, and the sheer vigour of this, a nursery rhyme published in the 1999 *Oxford Book of English Verse*, the first of three cumulative poems:

This is the house that Jack built
This is the malt
That lay in the house that Jack built.

This is the rat
That ate the malt
That lay in the house that Jack built.

This is the cat
That killed the rat

That ate the malt
That lay in the house that Jack built.

This is the dog
That worried the cat
That killed the rat
That ate the malt
That lay in the house that Jack built.

This is the cow with the crumpled horn
That tossed the dog
That worried the cat
That killed the rat
That ate the malt
That lay in the house that Jack built.

This is the maiden all forlorn
That milked the cow with the crumpled horn
That tossed the dog
That worried the cat
That killed the rat
That ate the malt
That lay in the house that Jack built.

This is the man all tattered and torn
That kissed the maiden all forlorn
That milked the cow with the crumpled horn
That tossed the dog
That worried the cat
That killed the rat
That ate the malt
That lay in the house that Jack built.

This is the priest all shaven and shorn
That married the man all tattered and torn
That kissed the maiden all forlorn
That milked the cow with the crumpled horn
That tossed the dog

That worried the cat
That killed the rat
That ate the malt
That lay in the house that Jack built.

This is the cock that crowed in the morn
That waked the priest all shaven and shorn
That married the man all tattered and torn
That kissed the maiden all forlorn
That milked the cow with the crumpled horn
That tossed the dog
That worried the cat
That killed the rat
That ate the malt
That lay in the house that Jack built.

This is the farmer sowing his corn
That kept the cock that crowed in the morn
That waked the priest all shaven and shorn
That married the man all tattered and torn
That kissed the maiden all forlorn
That milked the cow with the crumpled horn
That tossed the dog
That worried the cat
That killed the rat
That ate the malt
That lay in the house that Jack built.

(Anon eighteenth/nineteenth century)

This kind of verse is usually called 'folk poetry'. It's a dubious term, but it seems necessary, much as 'folk music' has seemed necessary for decades, and much as 'world music' seems now. All poetry, all music, I want to respond irritably, is made by folk, and all the folk are in the world. To define what is meant, I am pushed into thinking of negatives. 'This is the house that Jack built' and the two poems that follow seem to be free of the influence of the academy; or of any 'great' poetry. Without being in any way indecent, 'This is the house that Jack built' is not quite respectable. One cannot imagine any of Jane Austen's characters reciting it, at least in public. It has not been touched by upper class life. The rhymes ('cat/rat', 'malt/built') are like song rhymes, either conventional and obvious on the one hand, or rough and ready on the other. It is almost as though some singer of a lost tune has made up the words as s/he went along.

To be more positive, a great whiff of democracy ascends from it. It is hard not to speculate about what it was written for: to entertain, certainly, and to my ears (and to children's ears, I know from experience) it still does. But in what way? I can imagine it being said in the room of the houses of the rural poor as children went to sleep. But I can also imagine it said in the tavern, with a solo verse intoning the first line to applause, much as US audiences always greet the crooner's biggest; then the whole rising in a crescendo until everybody is reciting, more or less soberly, the last verse, and bursting out in laughter and further clapping and cheering at the end.

From the vantage point of the twenty-first century, we glimpse farming life of some one and a half centuries ago: not the life of the landowner, of course. Families – usually the wife and mother – made the household's beer, so there's the malt. Most homes were infested with rats, always to be watched in case they eat the malt. And both 'the man all tattered and torn' and 'maiden all forlorn' are easy to picture: the courting couple that became the mother and father of this scene. The priest is not one of Jane Austen's comfortably off parsons. Her appalling Mr Collins from *Pride and Prejudice* would have nothing to do with this priest, and neither would Mr Slope (see pp.29–30).

I teach this poem first because it is entertaining and second because it leads to dramatic writing. This is an exercise often done best in pairs. I think it is important that each pair is arranged so that they are children perceived to be of different abilities.

Another folk poem that works in much the same way is this:

There was an old woman who swallowed a fly.
I don't know why
She swallowed a fly.
Perhaps she'll die.

There was an old woman who swallowed a spider
That wriggled and tiggled and tiggled inside her.
She swallowed the spider to catch the fly.

I dunno why
She swallowed the fly.
Perhaps she'll die.

I know an old woman who swallowed a bird.
How absurd! To swallow a bird!
She swallowed the bird to catch the spider
That wriggled and tiggled and tiggled inside her.
She swallowed the spider to catch the fly.
I dunno why
She swallowed the fly.
Perhaps she'll die.

I know an old woman who swallowed a cat.
Fancy that! To swallow a cat!
She swallowed the cat to catch the bird.
She swallowed the bird to catch the spider
That wriggled and tiggled and tiggled inside her.
She swallowed the spider to catch the fly.
I dunno why
She swallowed the fly.
Perhaps she'll die.

I know an old woman who swallowed a dog.
What a hog! To swallow a dog!
She swallowed the dog to catch the cat.
She swallowed the cat to catch the bird.
She swallowed the bird to catch the spider
That wriggled and tiggled and tiggled inside her.
She swallowed the spider to catch the fly.
I dunno why
She swallowed the fly.
Perhaps she'll die.

I know an old woman who swallowed a cow.
I dunno how
She swallowed a cow.
She swallowed the cow to catch the dog.

She swallowed the dog to catch the cat.
She swallowed the cat to catch the bird.
She swallowed the bird to catch the spider
That wriggled and tiggled and tiggled inside her.
She swallowed the spider to catch the fly.
I dunno why
She swallowed the fly.
Perhaps she'll die.

I know an old woman who swallowed a horse.
She's dead. Of course!

An American poem goes like this. It is also a folk song, and has been arranged by Aaron Copland:

I bought me a cat.
My cat pleased me.
I fed my cat under yonder tree.
My cat says 'Fiddle-I-fee'.

I bought me a duck.
My duck pleased me.
I fed my duck under yonder tree.
My duck says 'Quack! Quack!'
My cat says 'Fiddle-I-fee'.

I bought me a goose.
My goose pleased me.
I fed my goose under yonder tree.
My goose says 'Quork! Quork!'
My duck says 'Quack! Quack!'
My cat says 'Fiddle-I-fee'.

I bought me a hen.
My hen pleased me.
I fed my hen under yonder tree.
My hen says 'Shimmy-shack! Shimmy-shack!'
My goose says 'Quork! Quork!'

My duck says 'Quack! Quack!'
My cat says 'Fiddle-I-fee'.

I bought me a pig.
My pig pleased me.
I fed my pig under yonder tree.
My pig say 'Griffy-griffy!'
My hen says 'Shimmy-shack! Shimmy-shack!'
My goose says 'Quork! Quork!'
My duck says 'Quack! Quack!'
My cat says 'Fiddle-I-fee'.

I bought me a cow.
My cow pleased me.
I fed my cow under yonder tree.
My cow says 'Woarr, woarr!'
My pig says 'Griffy-griffy!'
My hen says 'Shimmy-shack! Shimmy-shack!'
My goose says 'Quork! Quork!'
My duck says 'Quack! Quack!'
My cat says 'Fiddle-I-fee'.

I bought me a horse.
My horse pleased me.
I fed my horse under yonder tree.
My horse says 'Neigh, Neigh!'
My cow says 'Woarr, woarr!'
My pig says 'Griffy-griffy!'
My hen says 'Shimmy-shack! Shimmy-shack!'
My goose says 'Quork! Quork!'
My duck says 'Quack! Quack!'
My cat says 'Fiddle-I-fee'.

I bought me a wife.
My wife pleased me.
I fed my wife under yonder tree.
My wife says 'Honey, Honey!'
My horse says 'Neigh, Neigh!'

My cow says 'Woarr, woarr!'
My pig says 'Griffy-griffy!'
My hen says 'Shimmy-shack! Shimmy-shack!'
My goose says 'Quork! Quork!'
My duck says 'Quack! Quack!'
My cat says 'Fiddle–I–fee'.

The following poem was supposed to be an example of those, but it isn't, not quite, even though it is inspired by them. It is by a group of six top juniors labelled as 'gifted writers'.

There was a grasshopper stuck in a tree.
It wriggled and wriggled but couldn't get free
And then the bird went to see . . .

Now the bird is stuck in a tree.
It flopped and flopped but couldn't get free.
Now there are two stuck in a tree,
Grasshopper, bird,
And then the meerkat went to see . . .

Now the meerkat is stuck in a tree.
It squeaked and squeaked but couldn't get free
Now there are three stuck in a tree
Grasshopper, bird, meerkat,
And then the monkey went to see . . .

Now the monkey is stuck in a tree.
It swung and swung but couldn't get free.
Now there are four stuck in a tree,
Grasshopper, bird, meerkat, monkey,
And then the gorilla went to see . . .

Now the gorilla is stuck in a tree.
It thumped its chest but couldn't get free.
Now there are five stuck in a tree,
Grasshopper, bird, meerkat, monkey, gorilla,
Then the tiger went to see . . .

Now the tiger is stuck in a tree.
It scratched and scratched but couldn't get free.
Now there are six stuck in a tree,
Grasshopper, bird, meerkat, monkey, gorilla, tiger,
Then the elephant went to see . . .

Now the elephant is stuck in a tree.
It swayed its trunk but couldn't get free.
Now there are seven stuck in a tree,
Grasshopper, bird, meerkat, monkey, gorilla, tiger, elephant,
Then the teacher went to see . . .

Now Mrs P is stuck in a tree.
She shouts so loud she breaks the tree
And everybody's free from the tree.

Grasshopper, bird, meerkat, monkey, gorilla, tiger, elephant, and Mrs P.
(Six children, all 10, working as a group)

Most children come across rhythm and its magic in babyhood:

This little piggy
This little piggy went to market
This little piggy stayed at home
This little piggy ate roast beef
This little piggy had none
And this little piggy went wee wee wee
All the way home.

Many a poem has been written as a present: hence the tradition of dedicating poems to lovers, friends and others. I ask children to write a rhyme based on this one for a baby brother, sister, cousin or friend. Because the child begins by linking the poem with someone (presumably) they love, there is extra motivation in producing something. It mustn't make sense (a pig eating roast beef?). I offered an example to some children in Stratford, East London:

This big cat ran to Walthamstow
This big cat cycled to Forest Gate
This big cat drove to Leytonstone
This big cat got the 69 to Stratford
And this little cat (called Marley) said, 'Stop!
Wait! Wait! Wait!'

I don't expect writing from this session to take my breath away. It is something enjoyable to play with, especially when there are children in the class who are not fluent with words. One seven-year-old lived on a farm, and composed this 'for my sister Belle' who was two. She dictated it to her LSA:

The goat on the farm bleated
The goat on the wall climbed
The goat in the field waited for his food
The goat on the lane got muddy
And the goat on the wall
Sailed away to the sky.

(Rachael 7)

But one 9-year-old did, indeed, take my breath away when she wrote this:

This little light shines like dynamite.
This little light shines like a crystal.
This little light shines like a princess.
This little light shines bright yellow.
This little light shines on me all through my life.

(Clare 9)

One myth children are necessarily familiar with concerns the potential dangers they face from adults. The myth is present in the media everyday, but it was present long before in the story of Red Riding Hood and the Wolf, who is, of course, an evil stranger in animal disguise; it's present in the adventures of Hansel and Gretel and the witch; and, in modern fictional terms, it's present in the White Witch in C.S. Lewis's Narnia stories early on in *The Lion, the Witch and the Wardrobe*, who plies Edmund with

Turkish Delight; and it's present in Mrs Coulter in Philip Pullman's *His Dark Materials* trilogy.

It is a wonderful fact that this subject can only be approached in schools through the medium of art, and poetry and fiction in particular. Those folk stories in the last paragraph are examples and so are examples from modern literature. But this has been a problem for centuries (presumably since the beginning of humanity's time on this planet). Here is a picture of potential child abuse from the eighteenth, or possibly nineteenth, century:

Meet-on-the-Road

'Now, where are you going child?'
Said Meet-on-the-Road.
'To school sir, to school sir'
Said Child-as-she-Stood.

'What have you got in your bag, child?'
Said Meet-on-the-Road.
'My dinner sir, my dinner'
Said Child-as-she-Stood.

'What have you got for your dinner, child?'
Said Meet-on-the-Road.
'Some brown bread and cheese, sir'
Said Child-as-she-Stood.

'Give me some, right now'
Said Meet-on-the-Road.
'I've little enough for myself, sir'
Said Child-as-she-Stood.

'What have you got that coat on for?'
Said Meet-on-the-Road.
'To keep the wind and chill from me, sir'
Said Child-as-she-Stood.

'I wish the wind would blow through you'
Said Meet-on-the-Road.

'Oh what a wish, what a wish!'
Said Child-as-she-Stood

'What are those bells ringing for?'
Said Meet-on-the-Road.
'To ring bad spirits home again, sir'
Said Child-as-she-Stood.

'Oh, then I must be going child'
Said Meet-on-the-Road.
'So fare you well, so fare you well'
Said Child-as-she-Stood

This makes a terrific performance poem, and leads to interesting discussion. 'Who is Meet-on-the-Road?' I ask the children for another mysterious figure for the child to meet, and I ask them to compose a new dialogue. Olivia thought, alliteratively, of 'disturbing Dennis', and made herself 'Child-as-she-Stood':

What are you standing there for?
Said disturbing Dennis.
I'm thinking
Said Olivia.

What are you thinking?
Said disturbing Dennis.
Thinking about vampire bats and rats
Said Olivia.

I'm hungry because you just said that
Said disturbing Dennis.
You're not going to eat me are you?
Said Olivia.

Oh man good idea
Said disturbing Dennis.
I'd better be going weirdo
Said Olivia.

Oy don't call me that
Said disturbing Dennis
Would you like to listen to some music?
Said Olivia.

OK
Said disturbing Dennis
There you go
Said Olivia.

Ahhhhhhhhhhh!
Said disturbing Dennis
It's too loud it hurts my ears
THE END.

(Olivia 9)

A plot develops neatly and unobtrusively through this poem. Olivia's mention of 'vampire bats and rats' makes Dennis hungry. The poem comes up to date with that piece of street slang, 'Weirdo'. And there's a satisfying and inventive happy ending with the loud music that defeats Dennis. Then, with that bald, capitalised statement 'THE END', Olivia tells her teacher, and me, that she's had enough now, and would like to get on with something else, maths, PE, Science . . . It's like the sentence 'And then she had her tea and went to bed' that very young children write when they have had enough, and that figures in so many children's stories. Max's tea was still hot, remember, after all his adventures in *Where the Wild Things Are*.

A spiritual: 'Motherless child'

Sometimes I feel like a motherless child,
Sometimes I feel like a motherless child,
Sometimes I feel like a motherless child,
A long ways from home,
A long ways from home.

Sometimes I feel like I'm almost gone,
Sometimes I feel like I'm almost gone,
Sometimes I feel like I'm almost gone,
A long ways from home,
A long ways from home.

These lines come from the tragic history of the African slaves shipped to the United States, and in their simplicity and restraint they convey an unfathomable sadness. I have included them here because all too frequently children's lives move through tragic phases, and these lines resonate like no other with them during periods of great pain. There are few enough examples of accessible poems that are about emotional bleakness.

Teachers and other adults in schools can almost always tell from a child's behaviour when something terrible has happened: a bereavement of a pet, may seem trivial to us, but it doesn't to the child who is carrying around what feels like an unendurable sense of loss. Occasionally, the children tell us about these events themselves. If it involves animals, they'll often tell us straightaway: 'a fox came into my garden last night, and killed all my chickens. He didn't eat them, he just killed them'.

This was from a six-year-old on the morning after Dunblane . . . News of human bereavements, and family breakdowns, often take longer to filter through: we just notice an unusual day off school, perhaps; a paleness, an unaccustomed sadness, a tendency to linger on the edge of the playground.

If a school has a culture of openness, a culture that values honesty, the writing lesson is often where children can reveal their terrible stories, their sadnesses, whether consciously or unconsciously. Angela, for example, aged 10, wrote in a lesson of mine 'In my magic box there is my Uncle Terry. He died last Thursday'; and then she burst into tears. Another child wrote to her teacher: 'You held my hand when my parents told me they were splitting up'. And, in a poetry lesson, this 11-year-old remembered what she still saw as a betrayal, the first time she'd been left with a babysitter without her parents telling her: 'Where was my Mum / When I needed her / when I was two? / At a party'.

It is an important part of the job of the teacher and the LSA to enable children to address the dark things, the nightmares, the glooms, the blues.[2] We have to prepare them to face sadness in their own lives and in the lives of members of their family. Sometimes they feel like motherless children, even when they are not; just as we do.

I attack this subject rather upbeat: after reading this spiritual in an appropriately sombre way I ask: 'Can anyone think of words connected with this feeling?' and I get: 'gloomy, depressed, sorrow, crying, weeping, unhappy, miserable' and similar. After a little play with thesauruses, we find less obvious and more vivid words: 'the blues, lamenting, grieving, moan, mourning, glum, disheartened, doleful' and others.

I point out to the children the simple structure of this Negro spiritual, and ask them to do some similar. I point out that, because of the repetition, there is little problem building four line stanzas; but also, by the same token, the lines have to be especially strong.

Sometimes I feel like a feather in the air,
Sometimes I feel like a feather in the air,
Sometimes I feel like a feather in the air,
And I spread my wings and fly,

I spread my wings and fly.

Sometimes I feel like an old broken leaf
Sometimes I feel like an old broken leaf
A long way from the tree
A long way from the tree

(Anon 11)

Sometimes I lie in my bedroom and I don't want to see anyone.
Sometimes I lie in my bedroom and I don't want to see anyone.
Sometimes I lie in my bedroom and I don't want to see anyone.
Except my old Teddy.

(Anon 9)

I wrote above that there are few poems accessible to young readers that deal with sadness. Two marvellous examples by Kit Wright do. They are in his 1978 book, details of which are given below.

- 'Grandad' is about a bereavement. I over-simplify by saying that 'All of the morning' is about sadness: it is a simple poem that goes very deep into feeling of alone-ness.

4

More from the voice of anonymous: ballads

'John Randall' and 'Henry my Son'

Here's a poem – or perhaps a pair of poems – to talk about. It deals with hatred and murder, subjects from which we might be inclined to protect children. But if we do, we sell them short, because children hear about these things through the media almost every day of their lives and, of course, they think about them and worry about them. Poetry helps us, like no other subject except, arguably, Religious Education, to bring these things out into the open. I'm printing the poem in two versions. Version one, which is called 'John Randall', and sometimes 'Lord Randall' goes like this:

John Randall

Oh where have you been to, Lord Randall my son?
Oh where have you been to, my sweet pretty man?
I've been to my lady, Mother. Make my bed soon
For I'm wearied with hunting, and fain would lie down.

And what did she give you, Lord Randall my son?
And what did she give you, my sweet pretty man?
Eels fried in a pan, Mother. Make my bed soon
For I'm wearied with hunting, and fain would lie down.

What colour were they, Lord Randall my son?
What colour were they, my sweet pretty man?

All spickled and spackled, Mother. Make my bed soon
For I'm wearied with hunting, and fain would lie down.

What became of your bloodhounds, Lord Randall my son?
What became of your bloodhounds, Lord Randall my son?
They swelled and they died, Mother. Make my bed soon
For I'm wearied with hunting, and fain would lie down.

Oh I fear you are poisoned, Lord Randall my son.
I fear you are poisoned, my sweet pretty man.
Yes I am poisoned, Mother. Make my bed soon
For I'm wearied with hunting, and fain would lie down.

What'll you leave your lady, Lord Randall my son?
What'll you leave your lady, my sweet pretty man?
A rope for to hang her, mother. Mother, make my bed soon
For I'm wearied with hunting, and fain would lie down.

Here is version two, 'Henry my Son':

'Where have you been all the day,
Henry my son?
Where have you been all the day,
My handsome one?'

'In the woods, dear Mother,
In the woods, dear Mother.
Oh, Mother be quick
I'm going to be sick
And lay me down to die.'

'Oh what did you do in the woods,
Henry my boy?
What did you do in the woods,
My pride and joy?'

'Ate, dear Mother.
Ate, dear Mother.

Oh Mother be quick
I'm going to be sick
And lay me down to die'.

'Oh what did you eat in the woods,
Henry my son?
What did you eat in the woods,
My handsome one?'

'Eels, dear Mother.
Eels, dear Mother.
Oh Mother be quick
I'm going to be sick
And lay me down to die'.

I ask the children to compare these two versions of the same poem. Sometimes I do this with the whole class, but it is often more effective when the children, prompted by some questions, work in groups, while the teacher, LSAs and other adults circulate, listening in and adding new prompts.

In the first version, where is the first line that suggests to you that something wrong has happened? What word suggests that?

The fried eels were 'all spickled and spackled'. Individually, write a recipe for a meal that sounds, at first unpleasant, but then, much worse, threatening. Read your recipes to each other and make your meal sound as nasty as possible.

Compare the two versions.

What differences are there in the way the mother addresses her son? Why are these differences there?

What's in the first but not in the second? And what's in the second but not in the first?

What techniques do both versions have? (Repetition, rhyme, metre). Note that the second version lacks the climax the first version has.

I don't use these poems any more as stimuli for writing: I prefer to read them (and get the children to read them, too) first, for the sheer thrill they give, and second for the way they make the children talk about dark subjects.

For further resources on ballads:

- 'Why does your brand so drop wi'blood?' in *Come Hither* ed. Walter de la Mare

- Ballads can be found in many anthologies.

5

An anonymous alphabet

A was an Archer who shot at a frog.
B was a Blind man, led by a dog.
C was a Cutpurse who lived in disgrace.
D was a Drunkard who had a red face.
E was an Eater, a glutton was he.
F was a Fighter who fought with a flea.
G was a Giant who pulled down a house.
H was a Hunter who hunted a mouse.
I was an Ill man, hated by all.
K was a Knave who robbed great and small.
L was a Liar who told many lies.
M was a Madman who beat out his eyes.
N was a nobleman, nobly born.
O was a Ostler who stole horse's corn.
P was a Pedlar who sold many pins.
Q was a Quarreller who broke both his shins.
R was a Rogue who ran about town.
S was a sailor, a man of renown.
T was a tailor, knavishly bent.
U was a usurer, took ten per cent.
W was a writer, money he earned.
X was one Xenophon, prudent and learn'd.
Y was a Yeoman who worked for his bread.
And Z was one Zeno the Great. But he's dead.

(Seventeenth century)

The walls in the school where I'm teaching this don't display punctuation pyramids, lists of 'interesting adjectives and adverbs', or those suggestions for the beginnings of stories ('In a country long ago and far away . . .') that I've condemned as clichés earlier (p.16). Neither do they display alphabets. The classrooms are too full of celebrations of the children's abilities in the forms of their art, their writing, descriptions of their experiments. When the children in KS 1 are busy inventing an island, deciding its dimensions, working out its climate in terms of its place on the planet, discussing its geography, inventing its economy, they have no space for material designed by publishers and curriculum designers who have never met them; who have no idea what they are like.

I read this poem to the children. I told them that 'cutpurse' means 'thief', 'ill' here means 'wicked', not 'sick', that an 'ostler' groomed horses, and that a 'usurer' lent money at great interest. They needed no other help with the meanings. I told them about the alphabets I see in other schools, and asked them to make suggestions for one to go round the room. It mustn't, I said, be boring; so it mustn't, to say the least, start with 'A is for Apple'.

I made sure that the children didn't feel it was necessary to work through the alphabet. I felt that would be too much of a tiresome task, and not nearly enough of a labour of love. I didn't want the more fluent to worry about a line for 'B', say, when they had already thought of something for 'H', or even 'X'. I told them that I'd prefer them to choose the letters they most fancied. Nevertheless, two of the children attempted the whole exercise. They were both very quiet for over half an hour. I have not printed their worthy efforts here.

I started the lesson, as always, with conversation. One of the first suggestions was 'S was a servant who wore a hat', and it took only a moment or two of questioning to get the improved version: 'We need two more syllables, and a particular kind of hat'. Someone shot back 'S was a servant who wore a cloth cap' immediately. I suggested that some of the lines should be 'strange'. I mentioned alliteration, which surfaced in places. Although 'A was an Archer' is in rhyming couplets, I decided not to bring that constraint into the classroom, but made a note to experiment with it another time.

'F was Frankenstein who lost his bolt', the original line, cried out to be corrected to some pedant like me because, like almost everyone else, the child who contributed this believed that the monster was Frankenstein. I felt very smug about this, and also guilty, because the new version was metrically weaker. Maud, the girl who contributed 'K' was, it turned out, thinking of Midas, who received from the gods the gift of turning everything into gold with his touch. This provided a useful story with which to end the lesson. Maud developed the theme of wealth further: her contributions included 'L' and 'Y'.

'I' was contributed by Jenny, a member of staff, and it led to other adult contributions on the theme of developments in communication, such as 'E was an email who sneered at a letter' and 'O was an Olivetti that clattered and clattered'. The most off-the-wall lines, N, Q and R, all came from the same child, Isabel. I'm still thinking about the narrator who didn't tell a story.

Here is the complete class poem:

A was an awkward man who drank punch.

B was a butterfly who butted down a wall.

C was a comedian who sang a song.

D was a dragon who couldn't breathe fire.

E was an elephant who gave electric shocks.

F was Frankenstein's monster who lost his bolt.

G was a goblin who thought he was an elf.

H was Hannah Montana who rocks.

I was an inkwell that sulked by a computer.

J was a jigsaw we couldn't fix.

K was a king who loved gold.

L was a luxurious spa just over the road.

M was a motorway that shut down.

N was a narrator who didn't tell a story.

O was an octopus who ate a lot of oranges.

P was a pig that jumped up a jig.

Q is a queen who just lazes around.

R was a rota that was useless because it wrote down all the wrong things.

S was a servant who wore a cloth cap.

T is a tutu that teaches teachers.

U is useless, so we didn't ask it.

V was Venus who lit up.

W was a wasp that hated me.

X was an exercise man who couldn't do press-ups.

Y is a yacht I own down in the shipyard.

Z was a zombie who couldn't skateboard.

(Mixed group, aged 8–9)

One child was new to the school, and she hadn't written anything in my lesson the previous week when I'd first met her. But I'd made a special effort to get to know her, and had written down some of her words and read them to the rest of the class. This time she did write, the page arranged landscape-wise rather than portrait, in large angular capitals. The spelling had enough consonants and vowels in the right places to enable me to interpret it. She had clearly been turned on by the exercise. Her B line I took as a compliment for her new school:

> M was a mouse who went to a farm.
> B was a book that inspired someone to read.
> L was a light that went out.
> F was a field that fell in the river.
> P was a parrot who flew over the whole world.

(Mia 8)

Other ideas:

• Compare with conventional alphabets.

6

Anonymous speaks from the grave: epitaphs

Here lies the body of Benny
My fat beloved hamster.
He has now climbed his last tube
And probably regrets being fat.

(10-year-old)

I mentioned earlier four difficulties that I believe surround the teaching of poetry (pp.77–80). The most serious, by a long way, is obvious. Most people, including most teachers, don't like it. Some even hate it. And if you eat a vegetarian meal cooked by someone who doesn't like vegetables, or who even hates them, you will, however good the wine and the company, eat a bad meal.

Hatred of poetry is an oddity. I am passionate about architecture – not just great buildings, but houses and shops, museums and football stadiums. And nobody ever says to me 'I hate buildings'. They are bored when I say, 'Look at that spire!' but they don't hate it. People often express to me indifference about food (I am passionate about that, too) but nobody ever says 'I hate food'.

I have identified one root of a hatred even, of poetry. It's a belief that poetry can only be about Love, Loss and Death, and that it should assume full morning dress in the form of antique diction ('thee', 'thou' and 'verdant pastures') and capital letters when addressing these matters. And connected, somehow, to that is the assumption that poetry can't be funny.

In the folk poetry that we can find in almost any churchyard, jokes and Death figure largely. There, among the stones, among the grandiose, decaying, crumbling family monuments, hidden, often, by the unkempt grass, under the yew tree branches, there is nothing to affright the most garlic-bearing poetry avoider. These graveyard poems are like Clinton Card verses in one way: they weren't written by professional poets. They were written with irony, wit, and, sometimes, shining through the bitterness, true sentiment. And often the big cannons, Love, Loss and Death in the same places as jokes.

The playwright John Gay (1685–1732) wrote for his own gravestone:

Life is a jest; and all things show it.
I thought so once; but now I know it.

This anonymous example from Devon makes a belated democratic point from underneath the sod:

Here lie I by the chancel door;
They put me here because I was poor.
The further in, the more you pay,
But here lie I as snug as they.

This joke puts a commonsensical lay view of eternal truths wittily and hopefully:

Here lie I, Martin Elginbrodde:
Ha'e mercy o' my soul, Lord God,
As I wad do, were I Lord God
And ye were Martin Elginbrodde.

Some of these verses are probably nothing other than jokes. Though who can be sure?

Here lies John Bun.
He was killed by a gun.
His name was not Bun, but Wood
But Wood would not rhyme with gun, and Bun would.

And if this next one is a joke, it's a grim one. It's about a hanged sheep stealer:

Here lies the body of Thomas Kemp
Who lived by the wool and died by the hemp.

The pun in this one shows that this form of wordplay can be far from facetious. The parents who wrote it lived at a time (this must be explained to today's children) when 'Lettice' was a common name for girls:

Grim Death
To please her palate
Has taken my Lettice
To put in his salad.

Here's one of the best-known of epitaph gags. It's about a dentist:

Stranger tread this earth with gravity
Dentist Brown is filling his last cavity.

And then, a poignant, simple epitaph on a teacher:

School's out
Teacher has gone home.

I ask children to write an epitaph for a pet:

Here lies Stanley beloved cat
Smacker of pingpong balls when young
So they ricoche'd off skirting boards
O his strength all gone, all gone
Under this earth.

(Anon 12)

Or for someone who followed a particular trade, as in several of the above.

On a ballet dancer
No more pas de deux.
Her time at the barre is over,
her pointe shoes are pointless.

She has gone solo
and is a Sleeping Beauty.

(FS)

On a footballer

He has run his last midfield strategy,
Committed his last professional foul
Been shown his last card
And it's time for his last sending off.

(Jim 11)

These children seemed to relish the opportunity this idea gave them to be utterly unsentimental, not to say heartless. First, a lop-eared rabbit and two unlucky hamsters:

Here lies Mr Henry Heron.
He was an adorable lop.
He's munched his last carrot
And hopped his last hop.

(Emma 10)

I had a hamster called Ben
Who didn't like a poke.
I thought he was a great little one
Until he had a stroke!

(James 10)

Here lies the body of Benny
My fat beloved hamster.
He has now climbed his last tube
And probably regrets being fat.

(Kayleigh 10)

I asked Kayleigh about this. She said, blandly, to the amusement of the other children and to the mild discomfort of some of the adults, 'We found him stuck in one of his tubes and he was dead. We had to poke him out with a pencil'.

I am always pleased when other subjects they are learning about seep into my lessons:

Here lies the body
Of Ann Boleyn
Who met a gruesome end.
She was first among many
But Henry thought
It was time
To head off.

(Louis 10)

A poet wrote a moving epitaph for himself. It makes a perfect ending to the session of joyful, heartless clowning which the epitaphs quoted above usually comprises. I tell the children how Robert Louis Stevenson, the author of *Treasure Island* and *Kidnapped*, among other novels and many poems, was a sickly child and then a sickly man. He had been born in Scotland, and then he had travelled through Europe, hoping to improve his health. He found his favourite place in the southern seas, and died in Samoa, where he had lived for five years. The last three lines of this poem are inscribed on his tombstone:

Requiem

Under the wide and starry sky,
Dig the grave and let me lie.
Glad did I live and gladly die,
And I laid me down with a will.

This be the verse you grave for me:
Here he lies where he longed to be,
Home is the sailor, home from sea,
And the hunter home from the hill.

For more ideas on epitaphs:

• *Verse and Worse* by Arnold Silcock contains many good epitaphs.

7

And more from anonymous: riddles

One breath and lights out.

(10-year-old)

The riddle is a poetic form as old as any in our tradition, except possibly the epic. The Anglo-Saxons loved these tiny poems, and many are collected in *The New Exeter Book of Riddles*, a collection that was left by the first Bishop of Exeter, Leofric, to the cathedral library. In the introduction to his translation of this collection Kevin Crossley-Holland points out that the word 'riddle' has a nobler pedigree than we might think, stemming as it does from the Anglo-Saxon *raedan* which means, among other things, 'to advise, to counsel, to guide, to explain'. Connoisseurs of the sexual double entendre will find much to amuse in some of the *Exeter Book* riddles, though I have included none of them here: 25, 44 (though this is more a single entendre), 45 and 54 are four of them.

Here is Emily Roeves version of Riddle 69 in that book:

Among all things wonderful –
I saw this, most wonderful of all,
Water becoming bone.
 (Ice)

Here is an anonymous riddle which Crossley-Holland quotes:

In marble walls as white as milk,
Lined with a skin as soft as silk;

Within a fountain crystal clear,
A golden apple doth appear.
No doors there are to this stronghold –
Yet thieves break in to steal the gold.
  (Egg)

A modern poet, John Cotton, has a take on the same subject:

Within white seamless walls
I store my treasure,
A gold that nourishes.
Search as you will
You will find no opening in me.
Once shattered I am not for mending.

Jonathan Swift riddle may seem obscure, but the second version gives it away:

We are five little airy creatures,
All of different form and features,
One of us in glass is set;
One of us you'll find in jet;
T'other you may see in tin;
And the fourth a box within;
If the fifth you should pursue
It can never fly from you.

We are five little airy creatures,
All of different form and features,
One of us in glAss is set;
One of us you'll find in jEt;
T'other you may see in tIn;
And the fourth a bOx within;
If the fifth you should pursue
It can never fly from yoU.

I read the children those riddles, and some others written by teachers in groups on a course:

I am the eternal light,
a vibrant orange and golden as the sun.
I leap and pirouette
as if I were
the principal ballerina
on a never-ending stage.
I bring warmth
like the inflamed anger
of a person crossed
and I despatch darkness.
    (Fire)

I am an emerald umbrella
opening towards the clouds.
I leave my attire on the floor
prior to revealing
my new spring collection.
My less fashion-conscious relatives
wear the same outfit, year in, year out.

I am there the whole day through
(unseen by you)
drawing the face of the waves
in the midnight sky.
I melt like cheese
in the morning dew.
    (Deciduous tree)

And here's one more from John Cotton:

I am a see-through pear
Hanging from my treeless branch.
A bit of a conjurer, I can ripen suddenly,
Or disappear at the touch of a switch.
Like the apple I am good for you
Lengthening your days.
    (Lightbulb)

Children write riddles when they have grasped, first, that the speaker of the riddle is the answer; that the answer mustn't be obvious – that it is, in fact, more important to produce a striking poem than a riddle the other children can solve; and that a good riddle is something more interesting than the 'what is purple and cries in the night' variety. I remember – I was a smoker then – being chilled by this written by an eleven-year-old whose name I have lost:

> I am a killing machine.
> I roll around.
> I am a killing machine
> killing everyone
> who falls into my trap
> everyday.
> I strike and kill
> I am a killing machine.
> They think I am cool
> and I like that
> because they fall into my trap
> like that.
> They sell me in stores
> And I like that too.
> I am a killing machine.
>   (Cigarette)

Note that brilliant pun on 'roll', and the insistent repetition of 'kill'.

One group were studying the solar system, and they had also written haikus with the 5,7,5 syllable count. These poems work as riddles. I was happy to cash in on this previous learning, and pleased that my lesson had its context in what the teacher had already taught. It mattered little that the children were less strict about the haiku count as the lesson went on:

> Spectacular sparkling planet
> spinning like a miraculous
> misty moon.
>   (Venus)

(Alice 10)

This is a huge sphere
with one moon like a mirror.
We roam its surface.
   (Earth)

(Greville 10)

Biggest planet
famous for a big red spot.
Why doesn't he put some cream on it?
It's getting kind of public.
   (Jupiter)

(Jennifer 9)

A big ball playing
hula hoop with its rainbow
rings beyond Jupiter
   (Saturn)

(Laura 10)

Cold football in space
god of the dead, cold, icy.
One breath and lights out.
   (Pluto)

(Jenny 10)

Inspired in part by these children and their work, I wrote my own planet sequence. Leave out the titles, and they become riddles:

The planets
Mercury
You're speedy round
the track
like a god
(winged sandals hot on his heels)

Venus
A deadly furnace burns for ever under your acid
but in my dreams I see
a cool sister in a satin gown.

Earth

'If you don't (and soon)
start to look after me I'll die'.
(A voice growls from the sands and the soils and the seas.)

Mars

O planet of the deepest deeps
and the highest heights
can you hear the ice move and crackle
at your head and feet?

Jupiter

Greedy and rich in everything – and moons? –
come on, who needs sixteen? –
you and your family
could make up a solar system on your own!

Saturn

I have loved since a boy
to think of the seven rings
great Galileo Galilei saw
four hundred years ago.

Uranus

Another bling-lover
with your Shakespearean moons and rings
you lie on your side as if to show them off.
Is it true what Google's told me?
That under that rocky core
you're hiding trillions of diamonds?

Neptune

We don't know much . . . can't see too well . . .
a storm . . . some moons . . . how many . . .?
If Earth survives
one day

we'll find out.

If.

Pluto
The Big Friendly Giant would call you a 'not-mucher'
and we call you 'Titch', 'Diddy', 'Dwarf Planet' or,
in a kinder mood,
O Distant Traveller.

For more on riddles:

- Kevin Crossley-Holland and Lawrence Sail, eds (1999) *The New Exeter Book of Riddles*, London, Enitharmon. This has many excellent modern examples of the riddle.

8

Anonymous at Christmas

This poem is printed in Janet Adam Smith's anthology *The Faber Book of Children's Verse* and given as 'traditional', and that is why it is in this section of the book. Though there have been suggestions in recent years that it was written by a composer, Thomas Ford (1580–1648)

Yet if His Majesty, our sovereign Lord,
Should of his own accord
Friendly himself invite,
And say, 'I'll be your guest tomorrow night',
How should we stir ourselves, call and command
All hands to work! 'Let no man idle stand!
Set me fine Spanish tables in the hall;
See they be fitted all;
Let there be room to eat
And order taken that there want no meat.
See every sconce and candlestick made bright,
That without tapers they may give a light.
'Look to the presence: are the carpets spread,
The dazie o'er the head,
The cushions in the chairs,
And all the candles lighted on the stairs?
Perfume the chambers, and in any case
Let each man give attendance in his place!'
Thus, if a king were coming, we would do;
And 'twere good reason too;

For 'tis a duteous thing
To show all honour to an earthly king

. . .

But at the coming of the King of Heaven
All's set at six and seven;
We wallow in our sin,
Christ cannot find a chamber in the inn.
We entertain Him always like a stranger,
And, as at first, still lodge him in a manger.

I often read it to children before Christmas. Some words need glossing, of course, though the meanings of these words can be inferred from
the context. A sconce is a candlestick and a dazie is the hanging above a
throne.

The king is coming tonight.
We need to clean the house so it's sparkling.
Buy the food, roast chicken and salads.
Scrub the floors until they shine.
Plump the cushions, big and fat.
Mow the grass green and short.
Perfume the rooms, make his bedroom grand
Make the hallway welcoming.

The king is coming!
The king is coming next week!
I need to get to work
I need to clean
Clean clean
The cupboard doors
With soapy soapy
Water
I walk to the shop and decide
What I'm gonna have for dinner that day
So I buy
Chicken
Sprouts

Potatoes
And cheese
Next I get my suit
A white sparkly suit
With a black and white top
(now that ain't a surprise)
with black shiny leather shoes
but once and all I forgot
my silky white trousers
but now I have to buy a Dyson hoover
to hoover up my space
I have to buy a throne
For the King to eat his tea
Or I'm gonna get in trouble
Or maybe beheaded.

Henry VIII was on the wall, and that fact may have provoked that joke in the last line. Here is a very different piece:

The king is coming to tea tonight.
We need to clean the house so it's sparkling.
Buy the fruit, roast chicken and salads,
Scrub the floors until they shine.
Plumb the curtains, big and fat,
Mow the grass green and short,
Perfume the rooms, make his bedroom grand.
Make the hallway welcoming.
Hang up decorations, make the place gold,
Strip the beds and sofas and chairs,
Wash all the sheets and dishes,
Polish the shelves and television.
He'll be here very soon.
Everybody's getting nervous.
Will everything look OK?
Then I hear the doorbell ring.
The King is on his way.

(Anna 10)

The king is coming!

The king is coming
What shall we do?
Clean the house.
Come on you!

Hoover the floors,
Brush the sink,
Go out shopping
And don't stop for a drink!

Shop for vegetables,
Cook the stew,
Get the house sweet-smelling
Hullabaloo!

Polish the telly,
Polish the floor,
Paint the walls,
Paint the floor.

The king is coming,
That's what you do.
The house is ready,
Whew!

(Annabel 10)

For good joke poems about Christmas:

- 'The Computer's First Christmas Card' by Edwin Morgan (1990) (though note that his computer is a very early, pre-Windows, specimen. The poems come from a 1968 collection.)

- 'The Wicked Singers' by Kit Wright (1978)

And a poem about the central message of Christmas

- 'The Frozen Man' in the same book by Kit Wright.

9

How many miles to Babylon? A short anthology of anonymous poems

This is the Key of the Kingdom:
In that Kingdom there is a city;
In that city is a town;
In that town there is a street;
In that street there winds a lane;
In that lane there is a yard;
In that yard there is a house;
In that house there waits a room;
In that room an empty bed;
And on that bed a basket
A basket of sweet flowers.
Oranges and lemons

Flowers in a basket,
Basket on the bed;
Bed in the chamber;
Chamber in the house;
House in the weedy yard;
Yard in the winding lane;
Lane in the broad street;

Street in the high town;
Town in the city;
City in the Kingdom;
This is the Key of the Kingdom
Of this Kingdom this is the Key.

Oranges and Lemons

Oranges and lemons
Say the bells of St Clement's.

You owe me five farthings
Say the bells of St Martin's.

When will you pay me?
Say the bells of Old Bailey.

When I grow rich
Say the bells of Shoreditch.

When will that be?
Say the bells of Stepney.

I'm sure I don't know
Says the great bell of Bow.

Who killed Cock Robin?

Who killed Cock Robin?
I, said the Sparrow,
With my bow and arrow,
I killed Cock Robin.

Who saw him die?
I, said the Fly,
With my little eye,
I saw him die.

Who caught his blood?
I, said the Fish,

With my little dish,
I caught his blood.

Who'll make the shroud?
I, said the Beetle,
With my thread and needle,
I'll make the shroud.

Who'll dig his grave?
I, said the Owl,
With my pick and my shovel,
I'll dig his grave.

Who'll be the parson?
I, said the Rook,
With my little book,
I'll be the parson.

Who'll be the clerk?
I, said the Lark.
If it's not in the dark
I'll be the clerk.

Who'll be chief mourner?
I, said the Dove.
I mourn for my love
Who'll be chief mourner?

Who'll carry the coffin?
I, said the Kite,
If it's not through the night,
I'll carry the coffin.

Who'll bear the pall?
We, said the Wren,
Both the cock and the hen,
We'll bear the pall.

Who'll sing the psalm?
I, said the Thrush
As she sat on a bush,
I'll sing the psalm.

Who'll toll the bell?
I, said the Bull,
Because I can pull,
I'll toll the bell.

All the birds of the air
Fell a-sighing and a-sobbing
When they heard the bell toll
For poor Cock Robin.

See:

- Ted Hughes 'Leaves' in *Collected Poems for Children* for brilliant recycling of this form.

A man of words and not of deeds
Is like a garden full of weeds
And when the weeds begin to grow
It's like a garden full of snow
And when the snow begins to fall
It's like a bird upon a wall
And when the bird away does fly
It's like an eagle in the sky
And when the sky begins to roar
It's like a lion at your door
And when the door begins to crack
It's like a stick across your back
And when your back begins to smart
It's like a penknife in your heart
And when your heart begins to bleed
You're dead and dead and dead indeed.

I read this poem to children because, like all the best art, it is part of a preparation for life. The children partly know, or at least intuit, that they will, almost certainly, one day, suffer from the actions of an insincere person, whether a politician or a lover. It will hurt when it happens; when they hear this poem, they sense the potential horror, but actually can enjoy it. Some adults like horror films for the same generic reason.

Although this poem is usually printed with conventional punctuation, I have printed it in this form because the lack of punctuation emphasises the sense of growing terror.

How many miles to Babylon?
Three-score and ten.
Can I get there by candle-light?
Yes, and back again.
If your heels are nimble and light,
You may get there by candle-light.

For further ideas:

- Iona and Peter Opie *The Lore and Language of Schoolchildren*

- *The Oxford Nursery Rhyme Book*

- *The Singing Game*

These books are packed with marvellous material of this kind. Some of the songs in this book are close to the bone, like this one:

Silly old man, he walks alone
He walks alone, he walks alone;
Silly old man, he walks alone,
He wants a wife and he can't get one.

Or this:

The green leaves are falling,
Are falling, are falling,
The green leaves are falling,
Are falling for me.

Last night when we parted
She was nigh broken-hearted,
Isabella, Isabella,
Isabella for me.

Or this

Willie, Willie, waiting on you,
I shall no longer wait now;
Three times I have whistled on you –
Lovie, are you coming now?

They are all from the 1988 book.

Verse from the oral tradition leaks, to say the least, into written poetry, as I shall show in the next part of this book.

Writing to explore: poems from the written tradition

Introduction

I write as a way of exploring what I experience, and what I think and feel about that experience. I explore my emotions and attitudes and, of course, the language in which I express them . . .

John Cotton, private conversation

I hope that I have shown that we should not, whether as educators or as readers, dismiss poems from the oral tradition as 'childish'. That man in the wilderness; that stoneless cherry; that perfect, rolling, endless ring; that fish-pond 'all on fire'; that key, that kingdom; that quarreller who broke both his shins, that mysterious journey to Babylon and back . . . they all have, to my senses, in their contexts, the look, feel, sound, smell and taste of poetry. Because so many of these rhymes have links to childhood, and are therefore 'childlike' (a far cry from 'childish', of course), and because every teacher has been a child, I feel that they might be welcoming to those indifferent to poetry, and even to poetry-haters.

The border between traditional songs and poems on the one hand, and written poetry on the other, is not rigid. W.B. Yeats put a famous poem called 'Down by the Salley Gardens' in his first book, *Crossways*, published in 1889, but it was a traditional Irish song before Yeats wrote it down. His poem was an attempt to reconstruct an old song from three lines imperfectly remembered by an old peasant woman in County Sligo. Yeats recognised the poetry in the anonymous lines and, depending on your view of things, either purloined them, or put them in his first book in homage to the folk tradition. Yeats, then, was alert to the poetry of the ordinary people; we must thank him for that alertness, and we must thank even more that old peasant woman in County Sligo. Hardy had a similar experience with his poem 'The Colour', and was open about it (see pp.176–7).

Captain Cat in *Under Milk Wood* sings a song about Johnnie Crack, Flossie Snail and their unfortunate baby. Is this traditional material? Or Dylan Thomas's own? (1954). If Thomas made it up on his own, the oral tradition has informed the diction, the rhythm, and the spirit of the work. One can imagine a poet a hundred or so years ahead trying to make a poem of something, a rhyme that he heard his great grandmother say, a rhyme that I've printed on p.141.

> How far is it to Heaven, John?
> How far is it to go?
> Three thousand mile or more, my boy,
> As flies the blackened crow.
> Can we get there to sleep away
> Our troubles and cares?
> Yes, if you keep your hand to the plough
> And your eyes on the stars.

Both the maker of the original rhyme and the poet that I am imagining (and, rather presumptuously, writing for) a hundred or so years hence, are in the business of exploration.

Arriving now at the written tradition, I felt it would be more welcoming to my less enthusiastic readers (if any have got this far) to begin with some short poems.

1

Small explorations:
some short poems

'a fine field at dawn, horse-ploughed'

(Two 11-year-olds working together)

'Jays and mice and bluebells'

(7-year-old)

Although I have read poetry almost every day of my adult life, I still find, when I buy a new collection by a contemporary writer, I flip through it and read all the short poems first. I don't want to get involved in something that goes over a page or two, or three; at least not yet. 'Later', I find myself saying to that four-pager. 'I'll read you later'. And I do. But first I read all the short ones, often flipping the pages from back to front, despite the knowledge that the poet has designed his book – not just each individual poem, but the order of them – for a purpose. Later I'll read every poem, long and short, and in the right order, aware that a poem on, say, page 23, may well have information, factual or imaginative or stylistic, that may help my reading of the poem on page 24 – and other later pages as well. And that I will have missed these connections on my first reading.

If I, as an enthusiast, feel drawn to shorter pieces at first sight of a book, I am sure teachers less accustomed to, and less confident with, poetry will find the poems in this section welcoming. I hope so. So I begin this chapter with some lessons built on short poems.

Paul Keegan (2000) collects this poem by Thomas Lovell Beddoes (1803–1849) in *The New Penguin Book of English Verse*. There are poems that are shorter, but either I don't know them, or they are outside the remit of this book:

A lake

A lake
Is a river curled and asleep like a snake.

Short enough. A simple sentence. Write it out without the line breaks: 'A lake is a river curled and asleep like a snake'. It presents no serious challenge. It speaks to the geography teacher, should s/he care to listen: it brings into my mind those maps of meandering rivers, and their occasional ox-bow lakes that I had to study in my last serious brush with that subject. And it speaks to anyone who enjoys the countryside.

Small as it is, this poem punches far above its weight. I ask children to tell me the names of some of the poetical techniques that Beddoes uses. They readily offer metaphor ('. . . Is a river'), simile ('like a snake'), alliteration (those 'k' sounds), rhyme ('lake/snake') and, sometimes, questionably, personification.

I ask the children for other subjects they might write about, using some of these techniques. Between us, we come up with lists including the following and others: mirror, water, tree, cloud, wave, water, beach, street, moon, plant, sun . . .

But if a teacher is interested in linking his or her teaching of poetry to the current scientific topic, s/he might write up a list that might be based, first, on the current scientific or historical topic; and second, that he or she might draw suggestions from the children. Any science is full of such subjects, and I can imagine powerful short poems written to this model about, say 'electricity', 'gravity', 'force' and many others. Music works well, too: 'scale', 'harmony', 'cello'. In other words, this poem is a alley into the exploration of the world in which it lives.

And here are some examples of children's writing. They are exploring their language, and the way in which it might help them to understand natural phenomena of which they are fond: a wave, gorse, a rose, a cloud. All these children are in Years 5 or 6:

A wave
Is a dolphin diving into the water.

The gorse
Is gold thrown all over the heath.

A rose
Is a spiky sea urchin opening itself.

Two girls working together produced, with the help of a reference book:

A cirrus cloud
Is a fine field at dawn, horse-ploughed.

That poem was about science as well as art, of course, and the two children who wrote it had to refer to the library to find the word 'cirrus'.

When, eventually, I got around to widening the remit of this lesson to other subjects, children produced these. I have included some of their comments after each poem:

Gravity
Is an urge to take me down to the ground.

'I have got alliteration in there . . .' one child said, exposing an oddity: twenty-five years ago, almost no-one knew what alliteration is; now almost everyone leaving primary school does, as if it were a matter of life and death.

A note
Is a child on his own, lonely.

'I have some internal rhyme, "note . . . own . . . lonely"', said this writer, exposing here something almost no children know about. The 'note', the writer explained, was a musical one.

A melody
Is a line of infants playing with a long rope.

When this last was being written, the writer and I were watching reception children playing. I asked the writer to 'look, look, look – aren't you missing someone out? . . . Don't bother with those poetic techniques' and she added to her poem:

A melody
Is a line of infants playing with a long rope
With a dinner lady at each end.

Unison
Is a game with all the children.

I said at the beginning of this section that 'A Lake' was the shortest poem I knew that I could use in this book. But the early twentieth-century poet T.E. Hulme wrote a poem in one line which is worth reciting when looking at any elderly building: since I first came across it, I have found it impossible to look at a thatched cottage, a Georgian town house, or even my neighbours' late Victorian villas in the same way. As for Norman castles and medieval cathedrals . . . 'Old houses were scaffolding once / with workmen whistling' (published in Jones 1992).

All this has, of course, a resemblance to the haiku. It is winter. These children have written accounts of Christmas dinners (pp.40–43). Now they are writing little poems following the haiku example, but not fussing about the exact number of syllables. I had asked the children to mix things up: their senses, for example; and to find similes, comparing things to other things that didn't seem the same; and not to be afraid of repetition.

I could hear the clouds
Talking among themselves.

(Gabriella 7)

Clouds
The colour
Of pearl.

(Clare 8)

The final writer here, Briony, had given her teacher problems a year earlier. She said in this writing session to that teacher 'I was a brat in your class wasn't I?'

I could hear your mind
Speaking to me
Silently

(Bryony 9)

The next short poem is by Mary Coleridge:

> I had a boat, and the boat had wings;
> And I did dream that we went a flying
> Over the heads of queens and kings,
> Over the souls of dead and dying,
> Up among the stars and the great white rings,
> And where the Moon on her back is lying.

I taught this poem within a week of finding it in an anthology that W.H. Auden co-edited in 1935. I read it aloud to myself some twenty or thirty times first: the thought of reading any story or poem to children without preparation seems to me insulting, first to the story or the poem, and, second, to the children. I relished the dizzying updraft of Mary Coleridge's poem, from a boat on the water where it starts to, within six lines, the stars and the moon.

I asked Year 3 children to begin a poem with the line that was like 'I had a boat, and the boat had wings'; it had to have two different nouns: no boat, no wings. Here I was using the name of a part of speech in context: normally, 'noun' is only used in the dreary context of grammar lessons. I repeated that first line several times, emphasising its metre, and getting the children to follow me, phrase by phrase and line by line. Then I said: 'Obviously there was something magic about this boat . . . Can you close your eyes for a moment, and think of something magical that could take you somewhere?'

While I was reading and re-reading the poem and getting the children to play with it, Ria had half-internalised the rhythm. You don't have to be able to define 'rhythm' or 'metre' in order to feel them and even imitate particular examples. And this happens frequently, especially with strong traditional metres like the one that makes 'I remember' sing (see pp.164–65). Sitting at the back of the room with an entranced LSA watching her moving pen, Ria wrote:

> I had a flower and the flower grew power.
> It made me fly high in the sky.
> When I water my powerful flower it brings people back to life.
> When these people rose again they helped their families and very best friend.

(Ria 7)

She had noticed the rhyme, of course, and she made sure that she rhymed too: 'flower' led to 'power', obviously, and 'fly' to sky'. But less consciously, 'again', pronounced colloquially 'agen' in the last line, led to 'friend'. More interestingly, and even though I hadn't mentioned it, Ria had noticed, sub- or half-consciously, that steepling movement: Coleridge's poem took Ria from the rooted flower up to the sky.

Jessica just took off, writing so enthusiastically that there was no time for punctuation except at the end:

> I had a rocket and it drove to treeland I saw blossom trees and target trees and an ocean tree and a tree with patterns and a golden tree a bubble tree with a popping sound The tree I liked had a special name and the name was wagtail tree.
>
> (Jessica 7)

> I had a cat
> that could play the flute
> the most beautiful music
> you've ever heard
> about jays and mice and bluebells
> that can sing
> and last but not least
> it ran as it played
> attracting all humans
> through meadows and fields
> and cities and towns.
> The sun was bright
> But played until it old and stopped.
>
> (Safiyyah 7)

'Jays and mice and bluebells': much nonsense verse has arbitrary lists like this – for example, Lewis Carroll's 'shoes – and ships – and sealing wax – / . . . cabbages – and kings . . .' and Edward Lear's 'mince and slices of quince' and 'the runcible spoon' in 'The Owl and the Pussycat'.

Later, I made more of a point of the way the Coleridge poem flies upwards between the boat and the stars and the great white rings. This next writer was not fluent mechanically, and it took him some time to write this; but the last two lines make all the effort worthwhile, and I was encouraged how he took this point about the upthrust of the lines, and used it:

I had a hen
that could climb trees
and touch the stars
and brought one for me.

(Daniel 7)

I had a dog that could walk on two feet.
The dog could run but not eat.
He could walk, jog and sprint but he could not say 'Bon appetit'.

(Maud 7)

I asked this writer, 'What do those last two words mean?' and she replied, 'Dig in!'

My research turned up another Mary Coleridge poem:

The deserted house

There's no smoke in the chimney,
And the rain beats on the floor;
There's no glass in the window,
There's no wood in the door;
The heather grows behind the house,
And the sand lies before.

No hand hath trained the ivy,
The walls are gray and bare;
The boats upon the sea sail by,
Nor ever tarry there.
No beast of the field comes nigh,
Nor any bird of the air.

I asked a class of Year 5 and 6 children to think of any building that once was full of life, busy with fun or work, with games or laughter, but which now seemed to be dead. This meant that they should explore, mentally, or imaginatively, a building as it was in the past. Town centres these days seem to be dotted with dead shops, and I asked them to visit one in their imaginations; with what Hamlet calls 'their mind's eye'. Or, I suggested, they could think of a still living building – a shopping mall, a busy street, the school in which they are working – and ask them to visualise it as it might be in a few hundred years. Or they could describe, or picture in their imaginations, gardens where the 'ground [has] run wild', where there is a 'broken wall', where everything is 'abandoned to decay'.

I told them that I often visit old churches that used to be called 'redundant', but which are now more happily classed as 'historic', because the church no longer holds services in them. Standing in them I am sometimes conscious of ghosts: the stone steps have been worn down by how many people like me, just visitors, perhaps, but perhaps worshippers, and others with sadnesses in their hearts, and joys, and in either case prayers to pray. Sometimes old glass survives, and sometimes, sadly, memorial tablets to soldiers, for example, dead in wars.

English is this boy's second language:

An old house in Latvia
This huge house is wide.
The ceiling is cracking.
The floor is old.
The balcony does not have a fence.
The underground car park is rusty.
The kitchen is smelly.
There is nothing to do in it.

(Nikita 8)

I went to a home all crumbled and stony with rusty ladders and dusty walls. When I stept in the floorboards creaked there were holey umbrellas in a big pile I stept out again

(Lizzie 8)

There was once a house
Which had a scrumbly window.
It had some muddy curtains
Flowers died out
And when we knock at the door
We heard a creaky sound

(Jessica 8)

For more poems on the seasons:

- There are more short poems on the seasons' sessions (p.00).

Here is one more:

> What the Headteacher Said When He Saw Me Running Out of School at 1.15 p.m on 21 July Last Year to Buy an Ice Cream from Pellozzi's Van
> HEY!
>
> (FS)

One child imitated it:

> What my mum said when she knocked on my bedroom door, and I said 'Come in', and she came in and she looked around and I had tidied it.
> 'Wow!'

2

Hymn: exploring where the rhyme takes you

The leaves to the tree,
The waves to the shore
The clouds to the sky
And the rower to his oar.

(11-year-old)

I'll come to the hymn later. Indeed, I never say the word to the children: it would mean more or less nothing to most of them. First I ask them to compile a list of objects: 'What objects might send a Valentine card to what other objects?' Quickly, they come up with lines that are nothing special such as:

The blinds to the window,
The pencil to the pen,
The floor to the ceiling,
The door to the frame,
The picture to the paint . . .

And so on. I point out that their minds have stayed in the classroom, understandably, because their eyes have been roving round it. 'Let's take our minds outside', I suggest, and they come up with lines that are slightly more resonant:

The waves to the shore,
The leaves to the tree,
The sky to the clouds . . .

I suggest, 'Let's go further afield . . . where do you go on your holidays?'

> Roker to its beach,
> Cornwall to its cream,
> Paris to the Eiffel Tower,
> The lion to the zebra,
> The Sphinx to the pyramids . . .

Then I throw it even wider, and lines like these are called out:

> Saturn to its rings
> Mars to its redness
> The universe to its limit . . .

Sometimes I discuss that useful distinction between concrete and abstract nouns, and suggest that they might use some of the latter:

> The war to the peace,
> The hatred to the loving,
> The dream to the nightmare . . .

I then ask the children to compile as long a list as they can of lines like this. 'Mix them up. Make some nouns concrete, and some nouns abstract. 'Don't even look up until you've got at least fifteen!'

Now the trick is to show them that, inevitably, some of their lines will have ended in a word that is easy to rhyme in English: 'ee' rhymes, for example, are common (though you might point out that some of them are spelt 'ea' – 'sea' for example, and that some are spelt 'e' – 'he' and 'she' for two examples). Another common English rhyme is 'oo' – though sometimes it is written as 'ough' as in 'through' or 'ew' as in 'brew', 'new', 'stew' and 'crew'. Other easy rhymes for them to watch out for (in, of course, variant spellings) are 'ow' (both as in 'cow' and as in 'mow', 'one' (both as in 'throne' and 'bun') and 'out'. There are many more. I tell them:

> Choose one of your lines that ends with an easy rhyme, and make it line 4
> of four. Then decide what might rhyme with your chosen rhyme, and make
> it the end of line 2; decide what might send a Valentine to the object that
> you've put at the end of line 2, and make it the beginning of line 2; now

choose two favourite lines from the rest, with no rhyme at all, and make them lines 1 and 3. Don't worry about common sense: play with your lines, and see where the rhyme takes you. DON'T (I say emphatically) make lines 1 and 3 lines rhyme. And don't make the words within each line rhyme.

A child chose the line 'The waves to the shore', sensing that 'shore' might be easy to rhyme, which indeed it is. 'What rhymes with "shore"?', I asked. The child had probably never thought about rhyme, or at least not seriously, so I gave her a minute or two to think: most educational discourse lacks sufficient time for children to think. I stayed with her for a few seconds, but then said (putting her out of some misery, I suspect) 'I'll come back in a few minutes'. When I did, she had relaxed. She had thought. She offered 'oar', 'poor', 'core', 'four', 'door' and 'floor'. When she chose 'oar', I said, 'What might send a Valentine to an oar?' She immediately offered 'rower'. She then filled in the odd-numbered lines with favourites from her list, and came up with:

> The leaves to the tree,
> The waves to the shore,
> The clouds to the sky
> And the rower to his oar.

> (Gwen 11)

I called this section 'Hymn' because the traditional hymn offers us a simple way of, not so much teaching this, one of the oldest English stanza forms, but of explaining it to those teachers familiar with traditional Christian worship. The rhyme is ABCB: the odd-numbered lines (A and C) do not rhyme, the even-numbered lines (B and B) do:

> There is a green hill far away,
> Without a city wall,
> Where the dear Lord was crucified,
> Who died to save us all.

> (92 in the *New English Hymnal*)

Looking now at the hymn book, I notice that many hymns have an ABAB rhyme scheme. But I think that, if rhyme is garlic, this is too much garlic.

There are many ways of extending this. One is to ask the children to compose a stanza where all the objects are from the same sphere of knowledge:

The head to the toe,
The elbow to the knee,
The eyes to the ankle
And the body to me.

(Jimmy 9)

If I encourage them to choose a subject that is a passion, they will make better quatrains:

The cello to the violin,
The viola to the bass,
The unison to the harmony
And the tempo to the pace.

(Ravi 11)

Some children can vary the pattern, as in this poem of mine:

The thunder to the lightning

The thunder to the lightning,
  the wind to the tree,
the storm to the countryside, and
  danger, said the young boy,
    danger to me.

The forked tongue to the viper,
  the sting to the bee,
the eyes that look to distance, and
  danger, said the young man,
    danger to me.

Deceit to the deceiver,
  the imprisoned to the free,
life inside a loneliness, and

danger, said the old man,
   danger to me.

The sad song to the viper,
   the windward to the lee,
the boat to the beaching, and
   danger, then said everyone,
      danger to me.

(FS)

3

Exploring nonsense: Lewis Carroll

Jabberwocky

'Twas brillig, and the slithy toves
Did gyre and gimble in the wabe;
All mimsy were the borogoves,
And the mome raths outgrabe.

'Beware the Jabberwock, my son!
The jaws that bite, the claws that catch!
Beware the Jubjub bird, and shun
The frumious Bandersnatch!'

He took his vorpal sword in hand:
Long time the manxome foe he sought –
So rested he by the Tumtum tree,
And stood awhile in thought.

And, as in uffish thought he stood,
The Jabberwock, with eyes of flame,
Came whiffling through the tulgey wood,
And burbled as it came!

One, two! One, two! And through and through
The vorpal blade went snicker-snack!
He left it dead, and with its head
He went galumphing back.

'And hast thou slain the Jabberwock?
    Come to my arms, my beamish boy!
O frabjous day! Callooh! Callay!'
    He chortled in his joy.

'Twas brillig, and the slithy toves
    Did gyre and gimble in the wabe;
All mimsy were the borogoves,
    And the mome raths outgrabe.

I have written about this poem before (Sedgwick 2001). The obvious thing to do with these exuberant lines (from Chapter 1 of *Through the Looking Glass and What Alice Found There*) is to ask children to write other nonsense poems about weirdly named monsters; obvious, but dull. I have found that it is more fun, and more creative (in some contexts the words are close to being synonyms) to ask the children to make up dictionary style definitions for some of the nonsense words. I tell the children that any useful dictionary gives the reader more than what each word means. It also says what parts of speech it usually is, and even where the word comes from – its etymology.

The part of speech is a grey area, of course. Many words – most, possibly – change their part of speech depending on their context. 'Fast', for example is a noun in the sentence 'I am going on a fast next week'; an adjective in the sentence 'She is a fast runner'; and an adverb in the sentence 'I think fast'. I have a friend who deplored, during the last Olympics, the word 'medal' as a verb, as in 'Australia has medalled five times today'. But I never heard him object to the use of the noun 'picture' when used as a verb as in 'I picture you on a sunny day with flowers in your hair', or in the presumably ancient sentence 'I will milk the cows' ('milk' is usually a noun).

But all this adds interest to the exercise. For example, 'mimsy' was defined in three ways by a group of Durham teachers on a course. Each time, the members of the group saw it, or pretended to see it, as a different part of speech. I should add here that they had been asked to give an example of the use of the word:

Mimsy. Noun. A light black lacy undergarment, or a dress made in similar materials; neither usually worn with keeping warm the main requirement. 'Shall I get my mimsy, darling?'

Mimsy. adjective. A quality of a small child's complaints as seen by a parent while shopping, as in the following, spoken threateningly: 'Stop being so mimsy, Geraldine, or you know what will happen . . .'.

Mimsy. Verb. To be active without achieving much. One spouse to the other, while packing for a holiday: 'PLEASE do stop mimsying around and fold those shirts carefully'. Or one teacher to another: 'She [the head]'s been mimsying about at some meeting or other . . .'

Here are some definitions from children faced with the same exercise:

Tumtum. Noun. A tree that gives you fruit when you are hungry.
Tumtum. Verb spoken by babies when they want breakfast.
Borogove. Noun. A cave where something frightening might hide.
Slithy. Noun. A person I don't like.
Slithy. Adjective. Slippery.

4

Exploring the past: Thomas Hood

Fond memory brings the light
Of other days around me.

(Thomas Moore)

It is easy to be unaware that children aged 5 and over have a past, and a past that seems distant to them. Their first days at school, their early holidays, accidents and spells in hospital seem to them to be aeons away, but they can be suddenly brought up close and sharp with the help of poetry. This next poem is about the past and memories of it, and is one of the most powerful poems I know. My mother used to recite it to me; I have read it on my own hundreds of times; and I have read (or rather recited) it to children more than that, and yet it never loses its power. When I recite it, I watch children's faces, their feeling seduced by the first line with its repetition, by the lulling rhythm and the simple rhyme, and by its expression of the realities of a man's memories. I think more sensitive children are probably touched by its sadness: it is a dark poem: 'I often wish the night / Had borne my breath away'.

I remember, I remember
I remember, I remember,
The house where I was born,
The little window where the sun
Came peeping in at morn;
He never came a wink too soon,
Nor brought too long a day;

But now I often wish the night
Had borne my breath away!

I remember, I remember,
The roses, red and white,
The violets and the lily cups,
Those flowers made of light!
The lilacs where the robin built,
And my brother set
The laburnum on his birthday,
The tree is living yet!

I remember, I remember,
Where I was used to swing,
And thought the air must rush as fresh
To swallows on the wing;
My spirit flew in feathers then,
That is so heavy now,
And summer pools could hardly cool
The fever on my brow!

I remember, I remember,
The fir trees dark and high;
I used to think their slender tops
Were close against the sky:
It was a childish ignorance,
But now 'tis little joy
To know I'm farther off from heaven
Than when I was a boy!

I have worked with this poem many times, almost always with children at
the top end of the primary school. This time, I was with 7-year-olds. The
theme was 'Roots', and they were studying plants, and the teacher wanted
me to develop this in any way I thought possible. I asked the children to
think about their memories of earlier days, their roots:

I remember when my brother took my lolly when I was 2.
I remember when my mum's dad died.

I remember when I loved my doll my mum's doll Susan.
I remember my 4th birthday and Pippa my big brother's girlfriend bought
  me a motor bike it was a plastic motor bike.

(Kiri 7)

I remember when I was three and I went to Ghana with my mum and
  sister and my dad to see some more family.

(Baffour 7)

This boy, who is deaf and dumb, wrote that with help from an LSA and
signed it later to the whole class. Poetry is about more than words; it is also
about the way words bond us. As his hands moved, and as his helper translated, the warmth between him and the rest of the class was tangible.

Taria (7) wrote a long inconsequential poem about ordinary things, and
then put at the bottom something very far from inconsequential:

I remember when I was standing crying over my dad's dad in a little box.

If I wanted to put the case for this kind of writing as strongly as I could, I
would say nothing except to quote that line.

In a Key Stage 2 class, one child wrote:

I remember the goat on the wall. We thought he was going to fall.
But my dad said, goats are good at climbing on walls.
They don't fall.
And in the farmhouse we had vegetarian food and cider.
And my dad bought cider from farms, and he talked to the man who gave us
the cider, and he said, is it bad about the food and mouth, and the man said,
thank goodness for the cider, and my dad shook his hand.
And it was muddy and smelly.

(Jamie 9)

5

John Clare: 'Meet me in the green glen'

Meet me by the small park
  In front of the tall trees
Where there is no noise,
  Please come, please,

(9-year-old)

Love meet me in the green glen
  Beside the tall Elm tree
Where the Sweet briar smells so sweet agen
  There come wi me
    Meet me in the green glen

Meet at the sunset
  Down the green glen
Where we've often met
  By hawthorn tree and foxes den
    Meet me in the green glen

Meet me by the sheep pen
  Where briars smell at een
Meet me i the green glen
  Where white thorn shades are green
    Meet me in the green glen

Meet me in the green glen
  By sweet briar bushes there

Meet by your own sen
　　Where the wild thyme blossoms fair
　　　Meet me in the green glen

Meet by the sweet briar
　　By the mole hill swelling there
When the west glows like a fire
　　Gods crimson bed is there
　　　Meet me in the green glen

If this poem had been written by a child in a rural Northamptonshire school in the twenty-first century, the first comment that an inspector might make would be about its inconsistency in spelling, grammar and punctuation. Sometimes 'in' is given in the conventional way; sometimes it is given as 'i'; sometimes this child capitalises the 'Sweet briar', and sometimes he doesn't bother. This child bothers neither 'God' nor 'foxes' with a possessive apostrophe, and he doesn't punctuate at all.

John Clare (1793–1864) was such a child from rural Northamptonshire. Born into extreme poverty, he worked as a herder from childhood. He taught himself to read and write, and memorised the ballads his parents sang to him. He scribbled scraps of his own poems on discarded wrappings, and produced poems like this one from an early age. He became feted as an oddity in the London season, but thereafter his life was tragic. He was plagued with neglect, poverty and, eventually, insanity. He died in a mental asylum, aged 70.

I usually tell children something of this story, because it interests them, and presents them with an image of a poet which they have not come across before. Then, it is not difficult to get children to notice some of the poem's techniques. The most prominent vowel sound, as the children recognise immediately – you only have to ask them – is 'ee'. The poem glides rapidly as though on 'ee'– shaped skates. It is a crescendo: that great climax about 'Gods crimson bed' and the west '[glowing] like a fire' comes after a 'green glen': the poem has a similar movement to Mary Coleridge's 'I had a boat, and the boat had wings' (p.151) His lack of punctuation enacts an urgency. You have to say the poem as if it were a kind of chant. So, when I am teaching it, that's what I do.

I told the children that I had written a townee's version of this poem. It would be largely free of punctuation, too, both in homage to Clare, and also because I, like Clare, wanted a kind of chant effect. I said I would use alliteration instead of Clare's assonance:

Meet me by McDonald's
Near St Mary Tower
Where wanderers with mobile
Telephones and walkmen[1]
Whisper to their lovers
Meet me by McDonald's

Meet me by the jeweller's
Where romantics stare
At rings and precious stones
Emeralds and rubies
Where golds on purples shine
Meet me by the jewellers

Meet me by the bookshop
Where we've often met
To browse in books we couldn't buy
Poetry and painting
Story books Be there!
Meet me at the bookshop

Meet me in the evening
(Suddenly it's evening!)
After all the telephones'
Dull demented ringing
Love come with me
Meet me in the evening

Meet me in the Milestone
Where we've sometimes met
Over little glasses
Of the cheapest wine
Buying time alone
Meet me in the Milestone

The Clare poem always interests children. As I chant it, their eyes are on me, and their ears and their minds are on Clare's words. I say to them, think of a friend you want to meet. I ignore the religious/erotic/romantic aspects of the Clare, ('Gods crimson bed') though implicitly, of course, they hang in the air.

> Meet me in Cardinal Park
> In front of Frankie's and Benny's
> Where we'll munch and chat about actions and emotions
> We'll talk about problems a-many
> Meet me there
>
> Meet me in Cardinal Park
> At the cinema
> By the popcorn stand
> We'll enter the movie but you'll never seem so afar
> Meet me there
>
> Meet me in Cardinal Park
> In the car park
> My solemn speech leads you on
> It's time to depart
> Tomorrow, meet me

(Sophia 10)

I note the way that this next writer, like Ria anticipates adventures that she expects and party fears over the next few years.

> Meet me by the small park
> In front of the tall trees
> Where there is no noise,
> Please come, please,
> Come and climb a tree with me.
> Jump down and laugh and cry
> Then run away but never say goodbye.
> After that to the dirty lake.
> Look at the ducks and the brown broken benches behind

Then run to the top of the hill
And see what you can find.

(Priyanka 9)

Those children were members of a group of 'keen writers'. Certainly, they were all fluent with words. This next boy, on the other hand, hadn't been labelled such. He wasn't fluent with his words, and his writing emphasises something that I would, if I could, write in embossed capitals on the cover of this book and on all available policy documents about the teaching of literacy: poetry does not only speak to the 'keen' writers, but, given a chance, it speaks to everybody.

Stephen does not punctuate, as Clare didn't; and his poem, like Clare's, is full of feeling and observation; and Stephen has learnt from Clare as surely as Priyanka and Sophia have.

Meet me at Tasy Beck I can push you in Hope you can swim
Meet me down the corn field So we can feel the wind
when we sprint through Meet me at the camp fire
So we can roast marshmallows and watch all the colours of the rainbow
　　spitting out of the fire and smoke bellowing

(Stephen 10)

If I re-set this poem, lined conventionally, we get this:

Meet me at Tasy Beck
I can push you in
Hope you can swim
Meet me down the corn field
So we can feel the wind
when we sprint through
Meet me at the camp fire
So we can roast marshmallows
and watch all the colours of the rainbow
spitting out of the fire
and smoke bellowing

This is a picture-perfect image of boyish friendship.

6

Thomas Hardy: 'To the Moon'

I have heard the ponders
Of the person who wonders.

(9-year-old)

To the Moon

'What have you looked at, Moon,
   In your time,
Now long past your prime?'
'O, I have looked at, often looked at
   Sweet, sublime,
Sore things, shudderful, night and noon
   In my time.'

'What have you mused on, Moon,
   In your day,
So aloof, so far away?'
'O, I have mused on, often mused on
   Growth, decay,
Nations alive, dead, mad, aswoon,
   In my day!'

'Have you much wondered, Moon,
   On your rounds,
   Self-wrapt, beyond Earth's bounds?'
'Yea, I have wondered, often wondered

> At the sounds
> Reaching me of the human tune
> On my rounds.'

> 'What do you think of it, Moon,
> As you go?
> Is Life much, or no?'
> 'O, I think of it, often think of it
> As a show
> God ought surely to shut up soon,
> As I go.'

(Hardy 1976)

In spite of what anxieties, losses, boredoms and even terrors may have been inflicted on them, almost all children are optimists, and they have little in common with the dour heart-dried old genius who wrote this poem. Nevertheless, I decided, only last evening, to try it out in a classroom. The diction won't be a problem, I thought, and I was right. I read the poem once; then I read it again, asking them to yell when they heard a word that they didn't understand.

This was only an hour ago. Some children yelled at 'prime', 'sublime', 'shudderful', 'aswoon' and 'rounds'. I defined the first, second and fourth; explained that the third was, almost certainly, an invention of Hardy's; while 'rounds' was defined as 'orbits' by another member of the group.

The children were part of a group of keen writers whom I used to meet at 4.00 in the afternoon every afternoon for six weeks. I had got to know them fairly well, and they had begun to know me. I had asked them to write poems that were a dialogue between themselves and some extraterrestrial body. I had mentioned Hardy's rhyme and his alliteration, and, following the example of 'shudderful', I had permitted them one invented word in their poems. Chloe appeared to be an uncomplicated child who listened to everything with gratifying intensity and who, when the time came, settled down to work straightaway, disconnecting herself from any potential distractions. Watching her write, I felt she could have been in a study of her own rather than a buzzing classroom. I'm looking at a photocopy of her first draft as I type it up:

What have you seen up there Sun
In your day
I often pray.

It's not a lot.
I've seen everyone,
The fire of London, curious one,
I have seen the children sleep.

What have you heard up there Sun?
I hope you're not too far
To hear something
That should reach a star.

I've heard people scream for help
And I have heard the ponders
Of the person who wonders.

Who has tried to reach you Sun?
I know someone has died
On a misfortunate ride . . .

(Chloe 9)

None of these children had any serious chances to make second or third drafts, which is a shame. But this is an extraordinary document. Normally, I discourage rhyme, and although those rhymes that Chloe finds are far from perfect, they are better than those usually achieved by immature writers. Her made-up word, 'misfortunate', is somehow very Hardyesque; I thought this the second after I read it, but was not sure why, until, a few days later, I was walking, and a line of Hardy's came into my head: 'And the Atlantic dyed its levels with a dull misfeatured stain' ('Beeny Cliff'). 'Misfeatured': the expected negative prefix might have been 'ill-' but Hardy uses 'mis-', as Chloe uses 'mis-' instead of 'un-'. Chloe has found that Hardy's tone, his rhythm, even this eccentricity, has bled into her work. And the sun's address to the speaker – 'curious one' – is terrific.

Robbie, who was interested in all kinds of science, wrote

Oh black hole are you anything more than a dip to nowhere?
Yes I am a guardian of space's depths.

Oh black hole are you merry and bright?
No I even suck in light.

Oh black hole are you real?
Yes reality placed me here.

Oh black hole are you very horrorful?
Sometimes hell breaks loose.

Oh black hole are you a distructful force?
Yes nothing escapes.

Oh black hole are you alive
Yes I speak don't I – though I am your mind.

(Robbie 9)

Once again, I thought both Robbie's neologisms ('horrorful' and 'distructful') were well-chosen and Hardyesque. Shelby (whose poem isn't printed here) defined her invented words in a footnote at the bottom of the page: 'tambolendo' meant fun and excitement, which her sun never experienced; and 'mistcalogic' referred to a constant cold breeze. If, as W.H. Auden wrote (quoted in Brownjohn 1989) 'Imagination is the ability to name cats', we can glimpse it as well in the ability to invent new words.

All the children achieved something remarkable here, even if it was only one line: a sun, for example, that 'dreampt of many a thing / Pegasus flying with fragile wings'.

Another bleak little Hardy poem with a similar theme is

Waiting Both

A STAR looks down at me,
And says: 'Here I and you
Stand, each in our degree:
What do you mean to do, –
   Mean to do?'

I say: 'For all I know,
Wait, and let Time go by,
Till my change come.' – 'Just so,'
The star says: 'So mean I: –
So mean I.'

Next time I teach 'To the Moon', I will find a place for 'Waiting Both'.
For more on Hardy:

- Other poems by Thomas Hardy (none of them has any jokes) that
will move children include the following. I am going to print one,
because it both thrills and chills. Hardy wrote a note above it: 'The
following lines are partly original, partly remembered from a Wessex
folk-rhyme'. This reminds me of my story earlier about W.B. Yeats'
poem 'Down by the Salley Gardens' (p.145). Was that his poem? Or
someone else's?:

The Colour
'What shall I bring you?
Please will white do
Best for your wearing
   The long day through?'
'White is for weddings,
Weddings, weddings,
White is for weddings,
   And that won't do.'

'What shall I bring you?
Please will red do
Best for your wearing
   The long day through?'
'Red is for soldiers,
Soldiers, soldiers,
Red is for soldiers,
   And that won't do.'

'What shall I bring you?
Please will blue do

Best for your wearing
   The long day through?'
'Blue is for sailors,
Sailors, sailors
Blue is for sailors,
   And that won't do'.

'What shall I bring you?
Please will green do
Best for your wearing
   The long day through?'
'Green is for mayings,
Mayings, mayings,
Green is for mayings,
   and that won't do'.

'What shall I bring you
Then? Will black do
Best for your wearing
   The long day through?'
'Black is for mourning,
Mourning, mourning,
Black is for mourning,
   And black will do'.

7

Too wonderful for me: something from the Bible

things that I haven't got an inkling about

(9-year-old)

The Old Testament of the Bible contains many genres of literature. The first chapter of Genesis, up to the fourth verse of Chapter 2, deals with God creating the world; Deuteronomy and Leviticus are law; Kings and Chronicles, among other books, are history seen from one point of view. All written history is seen like that, of course: these books give the Israelites' view. Goodness knows how the Midianites or the Philistines viewed it all. The Song of Songs is an erotic poem, and the Psalms are also poetry.

There are three poems in Proverbs, Chapter 30 that can work with children. The first is in verses 18–19. Here it is in the King James Version (KJV) (though I have used the lineage from The New International Version (NIV), which makes it clear that this is poetry):

> There be three things which are too wonderful for me,
> yea, four, which I understand not:
> The way of an eagle in the air;
> The way of a serpent on the rock;
> The way of a ship in the midst of the sea;
> And the way of a man with a maid.

NIV gives 'too amazing' for 'too wonderful'. I collected some words from a class of Year 6 children that meant something like the KJV's 'too wonderful'. Some of the range of words that the children offered can be seen in these writings. Others were 'flummox', 'confuse', 'astonish':

> There are 3 things that puzzle me no 4 things that dazzle me
> 1. The way a girl thinks
> 2. If I will get a job
> 3. How old will I die
> and how do they make fish food.
>
> (Jamie 10)

I still enjoy Jamie's internal half-rhyme / alliteration 'puzzle / dazzle'.

> The three things that I haven't got an inkling about are . . .
> The way if you flick on a switch a light comes on straightaway
> The way the sun wants to go to sleep quicker in winter
> The way the stars only come out in winter
> And the way friends have a repeated laugh.
> (also the way a man shaves and the hair grows back and the way a book is
>   mesmerising)
>
> (Danielle 10)

Danielle explained that she meant by number five that each friend has a characteristic laugh.

> There are three things that befuddle me
> Four things that truly bewilder me
>
> A nocturnal animal's fear of day
> Life for those whose life is over
> The questions in someone's eyes when asking a question they're afraid to
>   be answered
> How the sun is sure to rise though nothing's certain
>
> (Ashleigh 10)

Later I came across this little poem by the American writer Richard Hovey, who lived from 1864 to 1900. He clearly treasured these Biblical lines as I do. He wrote

Secrets

Three secrets that were never said:
The stir of the sap in the spring,
The desire of a man to a maid,
The urge of a poet to sing.

Another Bible passage that I have used with children is this one, again given in the King James Version:

The wolf shall dwell with the lamb,
and the leopard shall lie down with the kid,
and the calf and the young lion and the fatling together;
and a little child shall lead them.

And the cow and the bear shall feed;
their young ones shall lie down together:
and the lion shall eat straw like the ox.

And the sucking child shall play on the hole of the asp,
and the weaned child shall put his hand on the cockatrice's den.

They shall not hurt or destroy in all my holy mountain:
for the earth shall be full of the knowledge of the Lord,
as the waters cover the sea.

(Isaiah 11: 6–9)

The following words may need a glossary: 'asp' is probably 'cobra', and 'cockatrice' 'viper' or 'adder'. I ask children to write their paradise poems. Sometimes I link this up with Caliban's speech in *The Tempest* (Act 3 Scene 2) that begins 'Be not afear'd, the isle is full of noises'.

8

Exploring Geoffrey Chaucer: a start

Her body was like a butterfly's
But without wings,
A pretty bug floating around.

(10-year-old)

He had a little trick –
He would back into a wall
And you would have a print of him on the wall.

(Another 10-year-old from the same class)

Geoffrey Chaucer (*c*.1342–1400) is easily the greatest poet in the English language before Shakespeare. Indeed, he can be considered the first. He is a bridge between Old English and the early Modern English of Shakespeare and his contemporaries. There is a case for believing, as I do, that children should, at the very least, be made familiar with a piece of his work. Of course his words look strange to us, but when we look at the beginning of his greatest work, *The Canterbury Tales*, we can see that much of the presumed difficulty is superficial:

Whan that Aprill with his shoures soote
The droghte of March hath perced to the roote,
And bathed every veyne in swich licour
Of which vertu engendred is the flour . . .

It is not difficult to see that here is April, with sweet showers piercing March's drought – Spring with all the goodness (virtue) that makes flowers grow.

In the Prologue to Chaucer's *The Canterbury Tales* we meet several pilgrims on their way from Southwark in east London to Canterbury to visit the shrine of Thomas Becket. They are a dubious lot. Some of them may be there for religious reasons; others may be out for a good time and others may be out to make money in dishonest ways. The miller is, in this company, an honest rogue. Chaucer introduces him in a wonderful passage that I use with children. When I teach this passage, I begin with Chaucer's five opening lines, so that the children have a flavour of his language, and then start again and then read the rest of the passage in my own prose version:

> The Millere was a stout carl for the nones;
> Full byg he was of brawn, and eek of bones;
> That proved wel, for over al ther he cam,
> At wrastlynge, he wold have alwey the ram.
> He was short-sholdred, brood and thikke knarre . . .

You must know that the miller was a big bloke, brawny and bony. Could prove it, too: he always won the prize at wrestling. Short-shouldered, broad, a thick fellow, he could heave off a door, or he could break it by running at it head first. His beard was as red as a sow or a fox, and broad, like a spade. On the end of his nose he had a wart, and on the wart there was a tuft of hair, red as the bristles in a sow's ear. His nostrils were black and wide. He had a sword and shield by his side. His mouth was as great as a huge furnace. He was a brawler and a buffoon, and his jokes were mostly filthy. He could steal corn, and treble his profit. Oh, he had a golden thumb! He wore a white coat with a blue hood. He was good on the bagpipes, and he led us out of town playing them.

When I read Chaucer's lines, I emphasise his use of hard consonants, 'b', for example: 'byg . . . brawn . . . bones . . . brood', and the force of the combination of 'thikke' and 'knarre'. It is easy to show that these consonants suit this bruiser of a man. I ask them to write a passage about another character in which the sounds of the words, as well as their meaning, suit the character they are describing. I offer examples of my own, a postman who was 'a nimble-footed man that nipped neatly round the garden gnomes'; or a teacher who 'ticks were ticked tidily, neat and nice'.

The flower Seller

The flower Seller was a very pretty lady,
Her hair was golden like the sun
Curled around her radiant face.
She was a small skinny woman
Aged about twenty-three.
Her face was like an angel's
But without a halo.
A holy friend drawn down from Heaven.
Her body was like a butterfly's
But without wings,
A pretty bug floating around.
Her nose was small
But her eyes were big
Bright blue and beautiful.
Her lips were as red as the roses she sold
And her voice was as clear as a bell.
She wore a pretty sky blue dress
And her shoes were always clean.
As she sold her flowers she used to hum a little tune
And she liked to tell me wonderful
Stories about mermaids in the sea
And princesses in castles.
I loved that flower seller.
She impressed me with her singing voice
And the poems that she told.
I loved that flower seller.

(Gemma 10)

This writer bravely decided to write about a character a million miles away from the brutal miller. She conveys childlike feminine delicacy with, among other things, the sounds of her consonants, her similes ('her body was a like a butterfly's / But without wings', with repetition ('pretty') and with an oxymoron, 'pretty bug'. I find the past tense in the line fourth from bottom ('I loved that flower seller') very sad. The sheer femininity of the whole piece, made as a reaction to something quite different, is amazing. The only false note, to my ear at least, is 'skinny' in the fourth line.

A boy composed something quite different, slowly, with much thought and no fluency, and he dictated it to his patient head teacher, who, rather than sit protected by her computer in her office, sat with him for over half an hour, and who then walked around and commented helpfully on everybody's work:

> The man's a wall of stone
> His clothes were blue and green
> As large as a house
> He could lift the heaviest weights.
> His face was like an ugly sister
> He had a little trick –
> He would back into a wall
> And you would have a print of him on the wall.
>
> (Daniel 10)

The power of what the children write with this stimulus still surprises me. They might be like Gemma, or they might be like Daniel; either way, Chaucer can still touch them.

9

Rupert Brooke's favourite things

Many of the most accessible poems are lists. One that I use often is by Rupert Brooke. It is 'The Great Lover', and here are two parts of it:

These I have loved:
White plates and cups, clean-gleaming,
Ringed with blue lines; and feathery, faery dust;
Wet roofs, beneath the lamp-light; the strong crust
Of friendly bread; and many-tasting food;
Rainbows; and the blue bitter smoke of wood;
And radiant raindrops couching in cool flowers;
And flowers themselves, that sway through sunny hours,
Dreaming of moths that drink them under the moon;
Then, the cool kindliness of sheets, that soon
Smooth away trouble; and the rough male kiss
Of blankers; grainy wood; live hair that is
Shining and free; blue-massing clouds; the keen
Unpassioned beauty of a great machine;
The benison of hot water; furs to touch;
The good smell of old clothes; and other such –
The comfortable smell of friendly fingers,
Hair's fragrance, and the musty reek that lingers
About dead leaves and last year's ferns

. . .

> Sleep; and high places; footprints in the dew;
> And oaks; and brown horse-chestnuts, glossy new;
> And new-peeled sticks; and shining pools on grass; –
> All these have been my loves . . .

The best text to link to this poem isn't another poem, but the song 'My favourite things' from the Rogers and Hammerstein musical *The Sound of Music*. I'd gladly quote it now (from memory, I'm not entirely proud to claim) but copyright is so strong on lyrics that I can't risk it. I tell the children that the poem should be full of favourite things that are quirky, possibly special to each individual: so no chocolate taste, no sounds of crowds after a goal, no cuddles from Mum and Dad. They are all too obvious.

> I have always loved
> The smell of lavender on my finger and thumb
> Pinched from my neighbour's garden
> And the view of strangers' back gardens
> Seen from a train.
> I have loved
> The sound of my father's keys in the front door
> And his Country and Western songs
> Playing from his room
> And the smell of onions frying
> And lying in bed on a Saturday morning
> Knowing I don't have to go to school.
> I love the moment
> When the front wheels of the plane leave the runway
> And almost straightaway
> We are in the air . . .
>
> (Alfie 10)

I don't know whether this writer was aware of how felicitous his use of 'pinched' is here.

10

A voice from the United States of America: Walt Whitman

Walt Whitman lived from 1819 to 1892, so he is almost an exact contemporary of Alfred Tennyson (1809–1892). But his poetry is like nothing that was being written in England at the time, and arguably children ought to be introduced to the sound of an authentic American voice:

I Hear America singing

I hear America singing, the varied carols I hear,
Those of mechanics, each one singing his as it should be blithe and strong,
The carpenter singing his as he measures his plank or beam,
The mason singing his as he makes ready for work, or leaves off work,
The boatman singing what belongs to him in his boat, the deckhand singing
　　on the steamboat deck,
The shoemaker singing as he sits on his bench, the hatter singing as he
　　stands,
The wood-cutter's song, the ploughboy's on his way in the morning, or at
　　the noon intermission or at sundown,
The delicious singing of the mother, or of the young wife at work, or of
　　the girl sewing or washing,
Each singing what belongs to him or her and to none else,
The day what belongs to the day – at night the party of young fellows,
　　robust, friendly,
Singing with open mouths their strong melodious songs.

I had never taught this poem before. Its confidence, expressed through those long Old Testament-influenced lines (the influence is the King James Version, so England is there!) and its utter lack of irony make it sound strange to some English readers, but these very qualities obviously appealed to the children. These 10-year-olds had had no experience of the USA, but they knew much about other parts of the world:

> I hear Ghana singing.
> I hear the corn coblett as it sizzles screaming help.
> I hear the sun shining like heaven.
> I hear the tragedy of funerals.
> I hear the joy of weddings.
> I hear the love of families.
> I hear the whispers of sorrow.
> I hear the ocean's winter breeze
> I hear pictures talk as they are hung.
> I hear the stars come out for me, and only me.
>
> (Michelle 9)

> I hear Nigeria singing
> I hear farmers singing sighs of tiredness
> I hear my soup singing a hymn ['song' crossed out here] of happiness
> I hear traditional outfits sing raps of boastfulness
> A workman sings praise of God.
> The rivers wave as I go by
> And the trees sway in my direction.
>
> (Nnenna 10)

> I hear the busy traffic of Nigeria
> I smell the blooming in the front garden
> I hear the great singing of my church choir
> I feel the warm hugs of Nigeria as it welcomes me.
>
> (John 10)

One other child, who, it turned out, had had wide experiences of other countries, chose to write about her house:

I can hear my house singing
I can hear my house singing warming me with its love
the tv blazing throughout the house as it screams with joy
I can hear the books singing a mystery behind each cover
I can hear the sun singing glistening through the world, it rays like steps of
   great joy
I can hear my house singing

(Lauren 10)

That school is in North London. The school that the following children attend is in rural Suffolk:

I hear Waxham singing,
The sea rumbling its tumbling song.
I hear the children chanting their melodic song at one with the sea.
I hear the fishermen singing, chanting up fish on their way.
I hear the sands singing silky and cold and ancient as time.
I hear the waves singing, bursting out with a fiery vengeance.
I hear the sky singing, perfect and blue and ready to pounce.
I hear the seals singing, laughing like a young hooligan.
I hear the sun singing, glowing and shining, a locked enigma.
I hear the horizon singing, beckoning me forward, hiding distant lands.
I hear the sand dune singing, solid and strong.

(Rory 10)

When gifted children write, they often write in a purple manner. 'Fiery vengeance', 'ready to pounce', 'like a young hooligan' are obvious examples here. In fact, Rory, who is truly gifted with words as with much else, is especially susceptible to this. See his writing on p.52 (section on *Treasure Island*). But we should be glad about this, because adolescence will come all too soon when many will become so self-conscious they'll hardly write at all, and certainly not read out what they produce to the rest of the class, as these children happily do. It is only disturbing when an adult writes like this.

I hear Southwold singing.
I hear the sea sing its songs of waves and sand
and the cannons sing of when they used to fire.

I hear the lighthouse sing of its light and its sheer white walls
and the beach sing of its rocks and its stones.
I hear the shops sing of their products.
I listen to the pier sing of its arcades.

(Robin 8)

And here is Louis from Tadcaster in Yorkshire:

I listen to York singing.
I hear the busy babble of tourists exploring the city walls.

I listen to York singing.
I hear the distant chime of bells signalling the time.

I listen to York singing.
I hear the metallic clang of steel against steel as the bells signal midday.

I listen to York singing.
I hear the ghostly clank of forgotten horses' hooves as they strike down
   again and again on the cobbles in the narrow Shambles.

I hear the excited chatter of children and mums hopping into one shop
   after another as the men lag behind.

I hear the wind whispering as swirls around the welcoming walls of the
   Minster.

(Louis 10)

11

Gerard Hopkins

The poet Gerard Hopkins (he is usually given his middle name, Manley, but he hated it, so I don't use it) was born in Stratford in 1844 when the place was an Essex village a few miles to the east of London. It was suitable for moderately successful businessmen, like his father, working in the city, which his father was. The house where he was born is long gone, but is marked by a huge lump of rock and an inscription outside the public library on The Grove. St John's Church, where he was baptised a few years after it was built, is still there, the middle of a lively, noisy town. Hopkins died in 1889.

This is the most accessible poem he wrote:

Pied Beauty

Glory be to God for dappled things—
    For skies of couple-colour as a brinded cow;
        For rose-moles all in stipple upon trout that swim;
Fresh-firecoal chestnut falls; finches' wings;
    Landscape plotted and pieced – fold, fallow, and plough;
        And all trades, their gear and tackle and trim.

All things counter, original, spare, strange;
Whatever is fickle, freckled (who knows how?)
    With swift, slow; sweet, sour; adazzle, dim;
        He fathers-forth whose beauty is past change:
           Praise him.

Hopkins loved things that were doubled – two-coloured cows, the wings of certain birds; he loved the patchwork look of fields and meadows seen from hills. In this context of 'doubleness', it is possible to get a grip, however tenuous, on the phrase 'Fresh-firecoal chestnut falls'. He also loved – and this appears slightly strangely here – the innocent tools of a trade. As indeed I do: the dirt-spattered spade and the fork of a gardener leaning against the wooden wall of an allotment shed for example. I imagine the instep over the blade part of these tools; or the mechanic's tools, or the carpenter's: screwdrivers, hammers, spirit levels. They take on a tiny fraction of the user's humanity. That is why a still life painting is not without humanity: someone has placed those apples there, with that cheese and wine, and someone will eat and drink them soon. Someone will carry that fork and spade out into the plot soon.

Hopkins praises God for these things in this poem, both before and after he lists them. I invite children to list things they might like to thank God for, offering them the chance to use the names 'Allah' or 'Nature'; or any other name they might think right: in Hopkins' part of London today there is a large majority of Muslim children.

I explain 'coupledom' as best I can. Quite often a child comes close to a good description of 'skies of couple-colour' – 'When you can see blue, but there are white clouds as well', for example. We talk about alliteration, which Hopkins uses powerfully in lines 4 and 5, internal rhyme and assonance, and the use of compound words ('rose-moles' and 'Fresh-firecoal'). And we play with that lovely line 'With swift, slow; sweet, sour; adazzle, dim'.

Sometimes when I teach this poem I link it up with Psalm 150 verses 3–6. The Authorised Version says:

> Praise him with the sound of the trumpet; praise him with the psaltery and the harp.
> Praise him with the timbrel and dance; praise him with stringed instruments and organs.
> Praise him upon the loud cymbals: praise hymn upon the high sounding cymbals.
> Let every thing that hath breath praise the Lord.
> Praise ye the Lord.

'Psaltery' is 'lute'; 'timbrel' is 'tambourine';

We have a powerful mixture here: the Authorised Version of the Bible, and Gerard Hopkins' poem. On this occasion, I didn't have time to quote the Bible passage:

Glory be to God for
The gorgeous green glass I glimpse in the sun,
For the deep dark dirt erning and churning as the worms wiggle in it,
For slugs sliding along the window,
For the slippery silver trail sliding along the pane . . .
Glory to God for everything.

(Aimee 9)

Glory be to God for the winter's whistle,
For the frozen leaves and chilly trees,
The crunch of the feet when the snow has fallen,
For the icy air and the shivering sleet . . .

(Jade 10)

Glory be to God for the wintry trees,
The fluffy snow crunching together,
The fat snow falling,
Flying snowballs side to side
The clouds twisting and turning, then they fall.
The dead leaves under the blanket of snow,
The cold air making it colder and colder.
The snow muffles all the sound,
The snow gets smaller like in a washing machine,
The snow's in the wash for another year.

(Oliver 10)

These three writers avoided the conventional images that children reach out for automatically unless taught not to – 'diving dolphins', 'hedgehogs hibernating cosily', 'cute animals', 'birds tweeting' and the like – and they surprised me. Aimee goes for images that not everyone would think beautiful and with her strong alliteration makes an arresting poem. Her invented word 'erning' almost earns its place, and it shows that Hopkins' example of internal rhyme had struck a chord in her mind. When Oliver had finished his first two lines, I chanced to read them, and I suggested that he should stick to the snow for his writing. He makes a little study of it, and a study, too, of words relevant to it. Look how the snow is 'fluffy' and 'fat'; how it 'crunches', 'falls', 'flies', and 'muffles', all in the space of a few lines; and his final washing machine image may be far-fetched, but it is a noble effort.

Appendix: a short anthology of poems on the seasons

The weather is, notoriously, an obsession with the British, and there are many poems that celebrate or complain about it.

The months of the year
January brings the snow;
Makes our feet and fingers glow.

February brings the rain,
Thaws the frozen ponds again.

March brings breezes loud and shrill,
Stirs the dancing daffodil.

April brings the primrose sweet.
Scatters daisies at our feet.

May brings flocks of pretty lambs,
Skipping by their fleecy dams.

June brings tulips, lilies, roses;
Fills the children's hands with posies.

Hot July brings cooling showers,
Apricots and gilly-flowers

August brings the sheaves of corn,
Then the Harvest home is borne.

Warm September brings the fruit,
Sportsmen then begin to shoot.

Fresh October brings the pheasant;
Then to gather nuts is pleasant.

Dull November brings the blast,
Then the leaves are falling fast.

Chill December brings the sleet,
Blazing fire and Christmas treat.

(Sara Coleridge)

After the fairly intense session in which the children had produced the 'Glory be to God' poems given above, I read this Sara Coleridge piece, a much lesser poem, of course, but a good light ending to a writing session on a winter day. We collected verses that the children had written. Three of them were contributed by adults in the classroom:

January so cold and bitter,
Mittens, gloves, hats and scarves.

February brings love to the world
And kisses go about.

March and the wind
Blows twigs off the swaying trees.
New born lambs in farms.

April
The beautiful cloudy air sweeps across the spring day.

May
We used to sit
Boy girl boy girl boy girl

Holding hands
Then dance
In a big ribboned circle.

June
And swimming pools are like fire alarms
But with excitement
While lazy adults
Relax in chairs.

July, all the sunbeds out,
No clouds at all.
Beaches and ice cream.
Or watching the tennis ball
Shoot down the court.

August
Crack!
The hard ball
Streaks to the boundary.
Polite English clapping.

September
Blazer a little too big,
Face polished, tie straight,
My little boy is off today
To 'Big School'.

In October ghosts and ghoulies come out
Stuffed with sweets.
Freaky Frankensteins
Knock on doors.

November sees
Bright dazzling fireworks.

December
Sledges speed down hills

Snowmen melt fast.
I'm off the sledge, rolling down the frightening hill.

under the crocus and catkin	the cherry blossom
under the cherry blossom	the heat of summer
under the heat of summer	the autumn damp
under the autumn damp	the winter chill
under the winter chill	the Christmas light
under the Christmas light	the Christmas light
the Christmas light	

(FS)

Three spring snapshot poems

Blossoms
All down the grass verges
bridesmaids in their pink and white
and pale green dresses.

Snowdrops
I am hopeful again:
a handful of tiny white bells
have pushed themselves like a miracle
from the cold earth.

Casting a clout
'Ne'er cast a clout till May is out'

(Old saying)

yesterday the sun shone
from breakfast until tea
and this morning I shove
my warm jumper in a high cupboard
until next October.

Summer
Summer is icumin in –
Lhudu sing cuccu!

Groweth sed and bloweth med
And springth the wude nu.
Sing, cuccu!
Awe bleteth after lomb,
Lhouth after calve cu,
Bulluc sterteth, bucke verteth.
Murie sing, cuccu!
Cuccu, cuccu,
Wel singes thu, cuccu!
Ne swik thu naver nu!

When I am teaching poetry, I like to use the environment, especially in its dramatic, temporary manifestations. There is pressure on all teachers to ignore what is going on outside the classroom. A storm crashes and flashes, but we are doing the Tudors or Victorian England, and Jon and others must go out into the corridor to see Mrs Someone-or-other, who comes in every week at this time (and has done so ever since she retired, or her husband died, or her children fled the nest) to Hear Children Read. The great West Indian cricketer Viv Richards came to this country aged nineteen to play club cricket. The first time he witnessed a storm, he once said on the radio, 'Man, I thought the world was going to end'. If he'd been at primary school at the time, he'd've been told, 'Stop looking out the window, Vivian, and get on with your Tudors worksheet'.

It's winter as I have been teaching lately, and as I am writing now.

You have driven to school, for example, with windscreen wipers on full pelt, and you lean forward as if that might help you see better. You listen to the weather reports, and there are cheerful voices warning you of danger.

This famous poem is a kind of anti-catalogue poem: it simply lists all the things that aren't around in November, especially if you live in a town.

November

No sun, no moon,
No morn, no noon,
No dawn, no dusk, no proper time of day,
No sky, no earthly view,
No distance looking blue,

No roads, no streets, no t'other side the way;
No end to any row,
No indication where the crescents go,
No top to any steeple,
No recognition of familiar people,
No courtesies for showing 'em,
No knowing 'em!
No travelling at all – no locomotion,
No inkling of the way – no notion,
'No go' – by land or ocean,
No mail, no post,
No news from any foreign coast,
No park, no ring, no afternoon gentility;
No company, no nobility,
No warmth, no cheerfulness, no healthful ease,
No comfortable feel in any member,
No shade, no shine, no butterflies, no bees,
No fruits, no flowers, no leaves, no birds,
No- Vember.

(Thomas Hood)

Another catalogue poem: signs of winter:

Three little poems for winter

Icing on earth's cake –
Underneath such rich fruit
Waiting for a birth.

The garden is a perfect page.
Let's print on it now
With boots and sledgerails.

Look at the hedge!
The white speckle hedge!
And the robin in there, hunting.

(FS)

Two further suggestions:

- 'Christmas Card' and 'The Warm and the Cold' *Collected Poems for Children* Ted Hughes

Goodnight

Here's a body – there's a bed!
There's a pillow – here's a head!
There's a curtain – here's a light!
There's a puff – and so good night!

(Thomas Hood)

Notes

Introduction

1 A back-formation is a shorter word derived from a longer one.

Introduction to Part II

1 The sad thing here is that the main reason a poet might lie in a poem isn't to deceive in the conventional sense, but because that poet has thought of a resounding line, had turned a neat phrase; and the result is so resounding, so neat, that the poet doesn't want to consider the truth because it may mean chopping the phrase away. Samuel Johnson's hyperbole has much to teach us if we want our words to be more than tinkling brass: 'Read over your compositions, and where ever you meet with a passage which you think is particularly fine, strike it out'.

2 It occurs to me suddenly, re-reading the above, that the education officer sensed that there was something dangerously magical about poetry. Well, there is.

3 Laurence Binyon 'For the Fallen': words said every Armistice Day all over the United Kingdom. The other rhyme comes from the nursery.

Part II Poetry

The voice of anonymous: poems from the oral tradition

1 It occurs to me now that I should have introduced the word 'caesura' here, the technical term for the pause around the middle of the line.

2 It is not, of course, our job to *make* them blue: we leave that to the

administrators of SATs, who shake our children up every few years by putting them in a meaningless race.

Writing to explore: poems from the written tradition

1   I know 'Walkman' is out of date! This poem was written in 2001, and, no, I'm not going to try to rejig it to bring in ipods.

References

Novels by Charlotte Brontë, Lewis Carroll, Roald Dahl, Charles Dickens, C.S. Lewis, Robert Louis Stevenson and Anthony Trollope are not included here because they are easy to find. I have not included a place of publication where it is obvious from the title.

Amis, Martin (2001) *The War Against Cliché*, London, Cape

Aubrey, John *Brief Lives* (2000) ed. John Buchanan-Brown, London, Penguin
This is a perfect train journey book for anyone who is interested, first, in what would now be called the celebrities of John Aubrey's time and before, and, second, gossip. Where else would one learn that a devout poet's wife was a showy wanton who drove him to an early grave?

Auden, W.H. and John Garrett (1935) *The Poet's Tongue*, London, Bell
This eccentric book, largely the work of the young poet/teacher W.H. Auden, never fails to throw up something interesting. Out of print, but well worth searching for.

Browning, Robert (1967) *A Choice of Browning's Verse*, selected and introduced by Edward Lucie-Smith, London, Faber

Brownjohn, Sandy (1989) *The Ability to Name Cats*, London, Hodder and Stoughton

Causley, Charles (1996) *Collected Poems for Children*, London, Macmillan
Causley, who died in 2003, was the finest English language poet for children the twentieth century produced, and there isn't a single dud in this collection.

Crossley-Holland, Kevin and Lawrence Sail, eds (1999) *The New Exeter Book of Riddles,* London, Enitharmon

de la Mare, Walter, ed. (1990) *Come Hither: A Family Treasury of Best-Loved Rhymes and Poems for Children*
Originally published in 1923, this book has a slightly quaint old-fashioned sub-title, but what I have said about Auden and Garrett (above) applies here, too. Time and again in this collection, as in the Opies' *Singing Game* (see below) one catches glimpses of the connection, often ignored, between poetry from the oral tradition and written poetry.

Duffy, Carol Ann (2007) *The Hat*, London, Faber
'The song collector', 'Rooty Tooty' and 'Mrs Hamilton's register' make this book by the Poet Laureate worth the cover price. Full of other gems, too.

Gardner, Helen, ed. (1972) *The New Oxford Book of English Verse*

Hardy, Thomas (1976) *The Complete Poems*, ed. James Gibson, London, Macmillan

Haughton, Hugh (1988) *The Chatto Book of Nonsense Poetry*, London, Chatto & Windus

Hughes, Ted (1963) *How the Whale Became,* London, Faber

Johnson, Samuel (1755: 1843) *Dictionary of the English Language*, ed. by Alexander Chalmers, London, Studio Editions

Jones, Peter (1992) *Imagist Poetry*, London, Penguin

Keegan, Paul, ed. (2000) *The New Penguin Book of English Verse*, London, Penguin

King, Clive (1963) *Stig of the Dump*, London, Puffin

Larkin, Philip (1988) *Collected Poems*, London, Faber

McWhorter, John H. (2001) *The Power of Babel: A Natural History of Language*, London, Heinemann

Morgan, Edwin (1990) *Collected Poems 1949–1987*, Manchester, Carcanet

Morpurgo, Michael (1994) *Arthur High King of Britain*, London, Egmont

Morpurgo, Michael (1996) *The Butterfly Lion*, London, HarperCollins

Newman, John Henry (1929) *The Idea of a University,* London: Longmans, Green

Opie, Iona and Peter (1955) *The Oxford Nursery Rhyme Book*

Opie, Iona and Peter (1959) *The Lore and Language of Schoolchildren*, Oxford University Press

Opie, Iona and Peter (1988) *The Singing Game*, Oxford University Press
These three collections are invaluable. The last, especially – see my note for *Come Hither* above.

Pound, Ezra (1934) *The ABC of Reading*, London, Faber

Ricks, Christopher (1999) *The Oxford Book of English Verse*

Rodgers, Marion Elizabeth (2005) *Mencken: The American Iconoclast*, Oxford University Press

Rossetti, Christina (1904) *The Poetical Works of*, ed. W.M. Rossetti, London, Macmillan

Sedgwick, Fred (1997) *Read my Mind,* London, RoutledgeFalmer

Sedgwick, Fred (1999) *Shakespeare and the Young Writer*, London, RoutledgeFalmer

Sedgwick, Fred (2000) *Jenny Kissed Me*, Birmingham, Questions Publishing

Sedgwick, Fred (2001) *Teaching Literacy: A Creative Approach*, London, Continuum

Sendak, Maurice (1963) *Where the Wild Things Are*, New York, Harper Collins

Silcock, Arnold (1952) *Verse and Worse*, London, Faber

Smith, Janet Adam (1953) *The Faber Book of Children's Verse,* London, Faber

Smith, Stevie (1975) *Collected Poems*, London, Penguin

Summerfield, Geoffrey, ed. (1970) *Junior Voices*, four books, London, Penguin

These books broke new ground when they came out, and they do not feel remotely out of date now. Often seen in second-hand bookshops.

Thomas, Dylan (1954) *Under Milk Wood*, London, Dent

Thomas, R.S. (1993) *Collected Poems 1945–1990*, London, Phoenix

Van Wolde, Ellen (1996) *Stories of the Beginning*, London, SCM Press

Wilde, Oscar (1993) *The Happy Prince and Other Stories*, London, Wordsworth

Wordsworth, Dorothy (1971) *The Grasmere Journals, The Alfoxden Journal*, ed. Mary Moorman, Oxford University Press

Wright, Kit (1978) *Rabbiting On*, London, Lions

Wright, Kit (1981) *Hot Dog*, London, Puffin

Wright, Kit (1994) *Great Snakes*, London, Viking

Wright, Kit (2009) *The Magic Box: Poems for Children*, London, Macmillan

Yeats, W.B. (1984) *The Poems: A New Edition*, London, Macmillan

Index